Community at Loose Ends

The Miami Theory Collective is based in the Department of French and Italian at Miami University in Oxford, Ohio, but also includes members from other areas of knowledge. For this volume on community the Collective includes James Creech, Mitchell Greenberg, Britton Harwood, Peggy Kamuf, Stephen Nimis, Marie-Claire Vallois, and Georges Van Den Abbeele.

Community
at Loose Ends

Edited by the
Miami Theory Collective

University of Minnesota Press
Minneapolis • Oxford

Published by the University of Minnesota Press
2037 University Avenue Southeast, Minneapolis, MN 55414
Printed in the United States of America on acid-free paper

Library of Congress Cataloging-in-Publication Data

Community at loose ends / edited by the Miami Theory Collective.
    p. cm.
  Includes bibliographical references (p.) and index.
  ISBN 0-8166-1921-2 (HC). — ISBN 0-8166-1922-0 (PB)
   1. Community life. 2. Community. 3. Community organization.
I. Miami Theory Collective (Oxford, Ohio)
HM131.C74285 1991   90-11131
307—dc20   CIP

A CIP catalog record for this book is available from the British Library

The University of Minnesota is an
equal-opportunity educator and employer.

Contents

.

Introduction

Georges Van Den Abbeele

What is the peculiar evocative force of the notion of community? What is its apparently irresistible attraction and ability to mobilize the energies of the most diverse groups, all of which are first and foremost constituted by their very interpellation *as* communities? Is there not an element of demagoguery or mystification at work in the seductive appeal to community that merits our critical scrutiny before we so quickly subscribe to its ideological prestige? Might there not be a way to analyze that element, to isolate and if possible to dislodge it, in order for us *critically* to evaluate the workings of different communities, and beyond that, to develop a more just logic of community?

Taking their cue from the all but universal use of the term community as an unquestioned value, the following essays seek to rethink what it is that *we* mean by community when both the New Left and the New Right claim for themselves the enthusiastic appeal the notion still garners. But if we mean to rethink what is meant by "community," this is neither to efface its putative last vestiges nor uncritically to endorse the blind utopianism it so often evokes. Instead, the urgency of contemporary appeals for a new *sense* of community, a new *sensus communis*, would seem to require a new concept of what it means to be together—that is, of the communal. And surprisingly, the West, as we shall see, is marked by a demonstrable paucity of ways to think community, although this paucity is perhaps less surprising when one considers the Western tradition's tendency to derive its disciplines and concepts from the presupposition of a self-generating subject. Before as well as after Descartes—that supreme thinker of autonomous selfhood—philosophy, theology, psychology, linguistics, and all the other *logoi* have attempted to explain the world by extrapolating its existence outward from the inner workings of a subject. The necessary originarity and self-engenderment of this subject suppose its radical independence from all objecthood, thereby embroiling it in a fundamental solipsism that ipso facto posits an insuperable obstacle to the ''alterity'' such thinking still wishes, or at least needs, to explain. The bankruptcy of this Western notion of an originary subjectivity is nowhere more poignantly to be viewed than in Edmund Husserl's famous fifth ''Cartesian Meditation,'' where the ''rigorous science'' of the phenomenologist cannot seem to prove the existence of anything or anyone besides his own eidetic self. Of course, the deconstruction of the theory of the subject has been the special province and pride of twentieth-century poststructuralism, and there is no particular need once again to rehearse its paradigms in this context.

Still, the very ''successes'' of deconstruction in taking apart the mystificatory constructs of the transcendental subject have led to its being accused of nihilism or of a willful (and irresponsible) delight in ''destroying'' any or all concepts of a general nature, including those that are said to be of benefit to progressive causes. Thus, according to this view, the category of ''the subject'' would be spirited away at the very historical moment that women, for example, and other oppressed groups have begun to claim for themselves the status and privilege of being subjects. Without responding here to the validity or invalidity of this particular charge, we would like to note that a similar view of poststructuralism as uniquely and irredeemably disintegrative in its interpretive effects would seem to foreclose any ability on its part to formulate a meaningful discourse about community. The celebrated claim that deconstruction is unable to come to terms with the sociopolitical, a claim unfortunately reinforced by the extreme caution exercised by some deconstructionists, leads to the charge that what politics it does have is at best quietistic and at worst reactionary in its witting or unwitting collusion within institutionalized structures of power.

Given such a climate, the deconstruction of community would appear insensitive if not pernicious in an age marked by the widespread apprehension that the ''old'' forms of collectivity are disappearing or have already disappeared, that impersonality, anonymity, and solitude are the lot of a modern humanity crowded into ever-expanding urban conglomerates, that the very bonds of social interaction are sundered by the multifarious dislocations, disruptions, and disappropriations that characterize life in postindustrial societies. For many, the celebration of difference and the suspicion of absolutes that characterize poststructuralism and postmodernism seem a mere ideological correlative of the ceaseless upheavals and relentlessly splintering effects exerted on the material level under modern capitalism.

Yet it is within this ambiance of vertiginous transformation and individualization that the call for a return to community has reemerged as both a necessity and a banality of contemporary political rhetoric, no matter what the persuasion. It is a necessity to the extent that at least a minimal claim of transpersonal relevance must be made if there is to be *any* politics at all (as opposed to some kind of universal solipsism), and it is a banality to the extent that the appeal to community is made regardless of party lines. To the left's investment in "community activism" as a strategic retreat designed to reconstruct and build anew a base of popular support in the wake of severe electoral defeats by the right in England and the United States, corresponds the Thatcherite and Reaganite discourse on the return of juridical and managerial responsibilities to the level of "local communities," a cynical euphemism for the dismantling of the welfare state at the hands of so-called private enterprise. Even the victory of moderate socialism in France was predicated upon the issues of *auto-gestion*, regionalist autonomy, and bureaucratic decentralization.

Some insight into the ecumenical appeal of community might be gained if we consider for a moment the difference between the two etymologies proposed by the *OED* for the word community, between the more philologically valid formation of the word from *com* + *munis* (that is, with the sense of being bound, obligated, or indebted together) and the more folk-etymological combination of *com* + *unus* (or what is together as one). But the stakes involved in choosing between a community that is mutual indebtedness and a community that is absorption into oneness are more than just philological. As if by coincidence, the rival etymologies point to the two classic ways the West has tried to theorize community, between the organicist notion of the "body politic" most colloquially linked with the name of Hobbes and the idea of social contract popularized by Locke and the Enlightenment *philosophes*.

Yet both of these theories are belied by the Western philosophical tradition's apparent inability to think beyond the subject as its organizing category. For the organicist, the social body must inevitably be ruled by a head (*chef* or *caput*) under whose leadership the members or membership are subsumed. The one who stands for the multitude is the familiar formula behind a host of authoritarianisms, from the absolutism of classical France through a plethora of modern forms of statism and totalitarianism. At its most nightmarish, the concomitant reduction of social differences is figured by the very emblem of fascism: so many rods fastened around an ax and from whose handle they become indistinguishable. As opposed to this essentialism that thinks the communal only at the risk of positing the state as subject, the notion of social contract assumes the *prior* constitution of self-determining subjects who "freely" aggregate to form a community. As idealistic as the capitalist ideology of the workplace *qua* locus of "free" exchange, with which it is contemporary and which brutally levels the difference between those who already own means of production and have goods to sell and those who have nothing to sell but their own labor power, the notion of social contract strategically forgets the differences between subjects that may obtain in such a way as to obviate, or at least complicate, the presumption of their absolute equality. In other words, to rephrase Orwell, some enter into the contract as more "equal" than others. Furthermore, theories of social contract have a hard time explaining from where and how these freely engaged subjectivities are constituted. This is because, once again, the social is thought from the standpoint of the individual who *then* encounters "others." As such, both organicist and contractual theories of community conceal the essentialism of a subject immanent to itself, which speaks either for and as a whole that would precede the parts (*com-unus*) or as a part that is itself already a whole before its encounter with other "parts" (*communis*). In their respective inabilities to think the communal relation as such and as the inaugural condition for the very subjectivities that claim to speak for it, the alternatives of atomism and totalitarianism have each proceeded to an aggressive reduction and elimination of social difference, which in turn has fueled the contemporary sense of the loss of community. Whether it be through the fascistic denial of difference pursued via the mechanisms of exclusion, deportation, and "final solution," or the bankruptcy of a possessive individualism whose celebration of the private and the personal in fact reduces all subjectivities to identical consumers of identical goods (whose sole variation stems from the economic necessity of creating ever-new markets for an [n]ever-saturated public), both of these forms of social essentialism vitiate the very condition of the communal relation, namely the *difference* between singular subjectivities which is part of what *they* share by being in common, even as those essentialisms take place in the name of preserving some mythic "community" (be it the Aryan race or the "silent majority" of Middle Americans).

Nor are fascism and possessive individualism the only discourses that conceive community as an immanent *com-unus*. The Christian doctrine of *communion*, as concretized in the sacrament of the Eucharist, looks back to the communal breaking and sharing of Christ's body *qua* bread and forward to that redemptive moment of eschatological commingling when the elect shall be reconciled and made one with God. This absolute communion is both the end of history and the end of the community whose redemptive narrative it is. Similarly, the traditional Marxist narrative posits the classless, propertyless society that *communism* would be, at and as the end of the history it would both recount and concretely bring about. And the liberalist ideal of *consensus*, most forcefully argued today by the works of Jürgen Habermas, narrativizes the end of the dialogic interchange that signals disagreement as the advent of a communal monologue, wherein the previously dissenting interlocutors would now speak as one. These idealized communities of consensus, communism, and communion are all predicated upon the utopian overcoming of the historical or agonistic differences that keep them from being at one with themselves, that keep them from being themselves. All three are thus subtended by a myth of immanence that would explain their coming into being as but the unraveling or disclosing of what already is, the underlying *com-unus* whose full revelation awaits the Second Coming, the Revolution, or the compromise of consensus. The providentialism of such a discourse clearly belies the claim to historicism since, theoretically speaking and as Hegel understood so well in the preface to the *Phenomenology*, history is already necessarily over if its end has been determined and if what remains before the end is but the inessential epiphenomenon of a time that can henceforth only be marked as dead.

Assuming, then, that no sociopolitical thinking can do without some theory of community, the urgency of rethinking that category requires the elaboration of a discourse that does not fall into the trap of an immanentism, whose pernicious effects have marked the political history of the twentieth century and whose preclusion of the value of difference makes it untenable before the contemporary exigency of articulating the demands of a host of new social movements (feminism, gay rights, ecological activism, and the struggles in support of the civil rights of blacks, Chicanos, Native Americans, and other oppressed groups— none of which movements are simply subsumable or even foreseeable under the traditional aegis of class struggle). It was in response to this theoretical climate that the Irvin Colloquium Committee of Miami University began in 1986 to organize a conference on various "postmodern" responses to the contemporary crisis of community. This conference, entitled "Community at Loose Ends," was held in the fall of 1988 and was preceded by two years of reading groups and seminars with the invited participation of Jean-Luc Nancy, Jean-François Lyotard, Ernesto Laclau, and Chantal Mouffe, all of whom also later spoke at the colloquium. Their contributions have been gathered in this volume along with those of other conference participants (Verena Andermatt Conley, Christopher Fynsk, Peggy Kamuf, Linda Singer, Paul Smith, Richard Terdiman, and myself). In the remainder of this introduction, I will detail the responses of our contributors to the communitarian crisis evoked in the preceding pages and comment upon the field charted out by their collaborative efforts, a field certainly not lacking in contradictions, gaps, redundancies, exclusions, and antagonisms. Far from seeking some metadiscursive resolution between representatives of poststructuralism, postmodernism, post-Marxism, and feminism, our hope (and it can never be any more than just a hope) is to clear a space so that the *necessary* dissonances of this theoretical community might resonate beyond at least the accustomed walls of academic strife.

The question of the institutional limits of any theoretical attempt to redirect the complex and multivalent signifier that is community is most explicitly addressed by Linda Singer in her contribution to this volume. Overtly situating herself in a contemporary or "postmodern" context as well as within the local and particular context of our collective work on the question of community, she critically and resolutely measures the ineradicable risks, complicities, compromises, and possibilities involved in a revisionist understanding of community as being "at loose ends.'' Only when it is acknowledged, argues Singer, that ''community is not a referential sign but a call or appeal'' to a collective *praxis* wherein we are all implicated ''emotionally and psychically as well as intellectually,'' can radically revisionist and antiauthoritarian struggles overcome the elitisms that plague the ''community of critical thinkers'' as well as any number of social movements, including that ''privileged progressive political narrative'' that is traditional Marxism.

A major focal point that organizes the work included in this volume is provided by Jean-Luc Nancy's *La Communauté désoeuvrée*, whose publication in 1986 first served as an impetus to our thinking about the question of community, and whose arguments are either explicitly or implicitly responded to by nearly every essay in this volume. In fact, our title of *Community at Loose Ends* can also be read as a ''loose'' translation of his *La Communauté désoeuvrée.*[1] Given the prominence of Nancy's book in the elaboration of the theoretical work of our contributors, and indeed already in the preceding pages, some detailed consideration of his text is in order.

La Communauté désoeuvrée takes up the question of community in a modern world where everywhere community has dissolved or been destroyed. This obvious failure of communal models is shown to be linked to their embrace of the notion of human *immanence*, that is, of totality, self-consciousness, self-presence. Nancy argues that such ''failed'' notions of community — communism, liberalism, Christianity, etc. — are tributary to a metaphysics that has largely been unable to think without recourse to the subject. (Thus, the importance for Nancy of the Heideggerian *Dasein*.)

Community, as Nancy wants to revive the notion, is neither a community of subjects, nor a promise of immanence, nor a communion of individuals in some higher or greater totality (a State, a nation, a People, etc.). It is not, most specifically, the product of any work or project; it is *not* a work, not a product of projected labor, not an *oeuvre*, but what is un-worked, *dés-oeuvré*. It *is* what is given and what happens to ''singular beings,'' the exhibiting or presenting of their singularity, which is to say, the copresenting of their *finitude* as the very basis or condition for their commonality. At its limit, the communal relation would be defined by something we necessarily all share and yet cannot communicate: death, which is but Nancy's hyperbolic metaphor of the day-to-day finitude that marks the singularities of our being. A community of finitude does not repair the finitude it exposes or communicates; it does not promise the recuperation of an infinity somewhere beyond our finitude, of a redemptive life after death. Rather, finitude is said to *com-paraître* (literally, ''to appear together,'' but also ''to be cited to appear before judgment''). This *comparution* would thus be more originary than any intersubjective link or any other social bond since the latter presuppose the prior existence of entities that can *then* be brought together, whereas the former marks the very liminality of our being together and being no more than together (of our being together *before* being even ourselves) in those incommunicable but necessarily shared moments of our finitude — of death, birth, and much else.

Pursuing his critique of immanent community on the level of discourse, Nancy locates a corollary in the language of myth, especially as it has been conceptualized from the Romantics through Lévi-Strauss, namely as the founding discourse of community. Myth, according to this view, is precisely what transmits itself from speaker to speaker as the myth of their communion, as the accession to itself — the performative enactment — of the very humanity that speaks it, as the immanence of a community of speakers ultimately founded upon the commonality of their speaking the myth of their own community. To the extent that myth accordingly communicates nothing but itself, it is not enough, says Nancy, to demythologize or demythify myth, not enough to say that "myth is a myth," since such reputed debunkings can do no more, in effect, than perpetuate myth in its very pragmatics of social foundationalism. Instead, argues Nancy, myth must be "interrupted," that is, disabled and displayed in its finitude as incomplete, exposed not as *oeuvre* but as *désoeuvré*. Such an interruption of myth is what Nancy calls "literature," by which he understands less some canon of aesthetically prized works of writing than all that which is communicated in the *comparution* of singular beings. Insofar as what is therein "communicated," however, is "not a message," but the *very* incommunicability of the finitude that is necessarily shared in community, this "communication" is necessarily never finished, can constitutionally never be completed as a "work," and thus itself occurs precisely *as* finitude. As opposed, then, to the always already completed work of myth (which can never say what it has not yet said), the interruption of myth that is "literature" takes place as "the inscription of our infinite resistance" (198) to the totalizing myth of immanent community, the irrepressible but unsublatable liminality of social interaction that is community at loose ends, or what Nancy calls in an eloquent and provocative turn of phrase, "literary communism."

In his essay "On Being-in-Common," included in this volume, Nancy pursues his exposition of the liminal logic of community while explicitly abandoning the expression "literary communism" because of "its equivocal character," which he says sounds too much like some "romantic literary society" or a "community of letters." Rearticulating the Heideggerian category of *Mitsein*, Nancy advocates a communitarian logic that would understand "that the 'mit' does not modify the 'sein,' . . . does not even qualify the 'Dasein,' but that it constitutes it essentially." Such a *Mit-da-sein* or *seindamit* would take place at a level prior to the relation between being and sense, or even prior to relation itself, for the term relation already appears too external and hence would correlatively presuppose an already-constituted interiority of being, for which any "relation" to the henceforth exterior world would occur as if a mere accident to its essence.

For Nancy, however, and still in a Heideggerian register, "essence is itself existence," necessarily finite and singular each time it occurs. To think community
"existentially," if you will, or non-essentially, then, is to admit that "there is no
communion, there is no common being, but there is being *in* common." If there
is no *sein* without *mit*, then "the question should be the community of being, and
not the being of community. Or if you prefer: the community of existence, and
not the essence of community." What Nancy is suggesting is that the challenge
of community is not to understand it in terms of some common being whose immanent exposition it would be, but rather to think the difficult but necessary
question of what the *in* of being *in* common means. And as Nancy further spec-
ifies, the philosophical consequences of such thinking are no less staggering:

> Once ontology becomes this logic of being in itself as being *to* itself, all
> ontology can be reduced to the *in*-common of the *unto*-itself. . . . The
> meaning of being is not common, and yet the *in*-common of being
> transperces all meaning. To put it in another way: existence *is* only in
> being partitioned and shared. But this partition, which we could call the
> "unto-itselfness" of existence, does not distribute a substance or a
> common meaning. It parcels out only the exposition of being, the
> declension of self, the faceless trembling of exposed identity: *we* are
> what it divides and parcels out.

What Nancy then locates as the task of exposing or expositing this *in* (whose
status as fundamental makes it radically unexposable) is not simply to engage in
"a description of the status quo" or even of "a kind of democratic noumenon
entrenched behind any sociopolitical phenomenon," a kind of zero-degree egalitarianism in the mutual encountering of our singularities: "It is nothing of the
kind. Whatever is not democracy either exposes nothing (tyranny, dictatorship),
or else presents an essence of being and of common meaning (totalitarian immanence). But democracy, for its part, exposes only that such an essence is inexposable." Rather, to expose the *in* of being in common is to enable thought itself
to "risk itself and abandon itself to 'community,' and 'community' to
'thought.'" It is to respond to what Nancy considers a categorical imperative,
common to both "philosophy" and "community," and "anterior to all morality
(but politically without ambiguity, for politics in this sense precedes all morality,
instead of succeeding it or accommodating it), a categorical imperative not to let
go of sense *in* common."

In her commentary on Nancy's text, Peggy Kamuf rehearses the difficulty of
pursuing such a logic of the limit, of thinking "on the limit." The difficulty is to
think the limit not as constrictive or restrictive but also as foundational, as the
very condition of possibility for such differences as those between proper and
improper, being and not-being, presentation and representation, or between the
exposition and the exposed. Commensurate with the philosophical difficulty of

exposing the inexposable *in* of "being-in-common" is then, as Kamuf suggests, the political one of displacing, through such a thought of or on the limit, "not just the idea of critique, but the idea of democracy. . . . Unless 'critique' and 'democracy' are or can be displaced names for each other."

Elaborating on another of Nancy's insights in *La Communauté désoeuvrée*, concerning the structural inaudibility of the testimony to the absence of community, Christopher Fynsk critically examines Richard Rorty's notion of "edification" to display its unexamined presuppositions: a consensus theory of community that ignores the disruptive effects of language in the singularity of its articulations and a critique of representation from which the subject of representation itself would nonetheless be "saved." Whence Rorty's liberalism and concomitantly "aggressive dismissals of discourses with a political agenda that seek to interrupt or exceed the horizon of signification." Articulating the concerns of Heidegger, Wittgenstein, and Benjamin, Fynsk then argues the urgency of a "politically effective language" that acts "as a kind of intervention in language by which the essence of language itself is brought into play." Concludes Fynsk, "When theory or criticism answers to language, they become a practice: the writing of community."

In deconstructing the essentialism and immanentism that command traditional concepts of community, the essays by Nancy, Kamuf, and Fynsk adumbrate the urgency of rethinking our notions of the social and the political on the basis of and from an understanding of community *as* limit or liminality, of rethinking them not from some abstract commonality but from the illimitable network of "loose ends" that mark the communitarian relation as what we necessarily already have *in* common.

It is by mobilizing such a thought of the limit that my essay seeks to rearticulate the concept of "communism," first denounced by Nancy as one of the chief examples of the myth of immanence, and then rehabilitated with the qualification of "literary" to designate the foundational liminality of community. Drawing heavily on Lyotard's reading of Kripke in *The Differend*, I focus on the name as the very *limit* of language to the extent that its "rigidly designative" function *across* the singularity of phrase universes does not exclude the ineradicable contingency with which one name can receive different meanings. It is this structural contingency that allows for the struggle over the meaning of a name to assume a political dimension. Questioning the validity of limiting this analysis to unambiguously proper names, I examine the case of a word at the very limit of the name, a word whose sense is also eminently rife with political contestation, and whose indefinite location between proper name and common noun is doubled by its evocation of a community where everything is held in common, namely "communism." With the help of Laclau and Mouffe's analysis of communist rhetoric, a communist "pragmatics" is delineated from the Popular Front practice of enumerating the names of its constituents, thus placing them in a relation of equivalence. It is this ''expansive logic of equivalence'' that defines communism as an ''egalitarian horizon,'' to which we can never fully accede, and whose name therefore also remains an irrevocable subject of differends, but whose critical unveiling of ever further levels of injustice works as a categorical imperative whose political import is not yet decided. On the other hand, the stifling of differends or the placing of checks on the expansion of equivalences risks the return of dangerous forms of immanence. The restrictive bounds of the nation-state are thus seen, for example, to deform many a struggle for autonomy into the exclusivist essentialism of local communities.

Lyotard's concept of the ''differend'' is thus seen to intersect productively with Nancy's insistence on finitude and liminality as the ground from which to think community, not as the tyranny of imposed consensus but as the very play of *differences* or ''loose ends'' that defines our being together, not necessarily as one (*com-unus*), but as our being both together and separate, as our being both together and apart even when we are together, as *our being in common precisely through the commonality of our differences.* For several years now, perhaps most visibly in *The Postmodern Condition* and in a series of polemics with Habermas, Lyotard has insisted upon the necessity to think the social bond today not in terms of consensus, but rather in terms of a dissension whose persistence is not to be seen as some kind of failed or flawed consensus whose demise is to be mourned but as the very stuff of politics, its pleasure and pain, its comedy and tragedy. *The Differend* is, no doubt, his most elaborate and rigorous inquiry into this question. By a differend, Lyotard means more than the regulatable debate or dispute that the word *différend* typically denotes in French, more even than a mutual set of misunderstandings that the Habermassian Band-Aid of dialogue could resolve; the differend is a disagreement so structured that its resolution in the idiom of one of the two parties (or even in the idiom of some third party) necessarily wrongs the other party. In other words, the differend is precisely that which *cannot* be reduced to a consensus, or what remains left out of a consensus and betrays what is really at stake in the disagreement, the very source or occasion of the dispute. As such, the ''resolution'' or aggravation of differends becomes a difficult political or ethical as well as philosophical issue. To borrow the example that motivates much of this book, that of the Nazi genocide of the Jews, the ''dispute'' between S.S. and deportees (if we can call it that by so unjustly anodyne an expression) is egregiously *not* something to be mediated through the compromise solution of a consensus, when the enormity of the Nazi crime is such as to obviate the very possibility of dialogue, whether by the physical extermination of the interlocutor, or by impugning the evidence of the survivor's testimony. Rather than the kind of community typified by National Socialism or by the Cashinahua Indians of South America and characterized by a mythic narration of itself as an exclusive humanity that intolerantly relegates all other humans to the status of the inhuman, the ethical and political ideal would be to establish a social arrangement that gives the differend "its due," either by the invention of new idioms that could phrase with justice the wrong that remains unarticulated or by acknowledging the justness of the differend's inability to be phrased. In any case, the ethical imperative guiding the philosopher, the "moral politician," even the artist, is to listen to what as yet remains inaudible beneath the sound and the fury of official politics, to the differend that remains smothered even, or especially, under the legal façade of litigation and the law.

Such a political *écoute* conjures up the image of the political philosopher as psychoanalyst of the community, and indeed in his contribution to this volume, Lyotard recodes the structured incommunicability and injustice of the differend in a register that also replaces the Heideggerian theme of finitude which informs Nancy's work with that of the Freudian unconscious as socially structuring agent. Written to commemorate the twentieth anniversary of May '68, "À l'insu (Unbeknownst)" is explicitly addressed to the unknown, to "the thing" that remains repressed by and "unbeknownst" to the polis, understood as the overtly political, civic, or legal apparatus of the social: the ego and superego of the community's "soul." As such, a political unconscious is formed by what the polis "forgets," and it must forget something, for it cannot possibly manage everything, which is what fascism delusionally tried to do even as it reproduced "within itself, in the anatomy and physiology of its national body politic, the illness that it claim[ed] to cure," that is, the inner schisms and vertiginous feuding hidden behind the totalitarian state's "delirium and arrogance." All politics, says Lyotard, is "a politics of forgetting," not because politics has some "intention to make forgotten," but by the structural necessity of what it can neither manage, treat, nor represent, and which henceforth persists as what Freud would call an "unconscious affect," and what Lyotard here calls "the thing." Not to be confused with some version of ideology or social imaginary, the "thing" is precisely what escapes politics and cannot be managed by it, yet what can return to it as what must be "absolutely gotten rid of" by its very unbearability and repulsiveness (which also constitute its attractiveness) to the political order that repressed it. Hence, its solicitation of "a kind of paranoia" in its uncanny return, which motivates the irrational energy of xenophobia, purges, denunciations, show trials, and final solutions. Yet all these attempts to manage or link this irrepressible thing onto the chain of politics "only inspires yet more unleashing." Revolutions, too, "are attempts to approach it, to make the community more faithful to what, unbeknownst to it, inhabits it," yet this fidelity of the revolution to the thing is also and necessarily an infidelity or betrayal of it by the "attempt to regulate, to suppress, to efface the effects that the thing engenders." Marxian revolution, for example, means a "fidelity to the non-enchained" creative energy of labor power before it would have been bound, chained, and exploited through the workplace contract as it occurs under "the capitalist organization of being together."

For Lyotard, the events of May '68 were marked by a similar fidelity to the thing— here childhood, understood not as "a collective infantile regression" nor as the primarily youthful age of its participants, but as the "childhood" of the mind, the "enigma that the mind existed 'before' existing" as conscious subject, the dispossession that preceded the earliest sense of one's self-possession, its "dependence." From the adult point of view, the wrong felt by childhood seems absurd, ridiculous, and certainly not deserving of "serious" attention. We thus have the situation of a differend, for the adult idiom cannot resolve the differend without wronging the child's: "In the mind, childhood is not happiness and innocence, but the state of dependency. Childhood itself seeks to rid itself of that state and become 'grown-up.' It does not give evidence of its irresponsibility as a self-flattery, but as a complaint. May '68 sighed the lament of an incurable suffering, the suffering of not having been born free." "Mourning" the impossibility of a revolution that would be absolutely faithful to the thing, recognizing that the return of official political discourse also marked the end of the May '68 events, that "politics will never be anything but the art of the possible," and that the West persists in "its work of managing the unmanageable [*traitement de l'intraitable*]," Lyotard's text would thus nonetheless seem to locate what is most momentously (and unpredictably) political precisely where (official) politics is not. As he asks, "Are there other politics—other than revolutionary—that would make it possible not to be unfaithful to the thing that inhabits the polis unconsciously?"

Such a question is subtended by an imperative of fidelity to the "otherness" of this thing, an imperative that implicitly adumbrates a primordiality of ethics over politics which recalls the work of Emmanuel Lévinas, a philosopher whose thought has determinately inflected Lyotard's reflections on the necessity of dissension within communities. Against the epistemological point of view that can know the other only by denying its otherness, Lévinas posits a radically different kind of relation grounded in the "face-to-face encounter with the other" as what precedes any epistemological reduction. Not simply knowable, but not for that matter impalpable, the intersubjective *situation* is inaugural of ethics, and by necessity, of any thought of community. Writing then in an explicitly situational and autobiographical mode, Verena Andermatt Conley reflects via image as well as word on the sweepingly disruptive effects postmodern economic and teleological relations are wreaking on communities of all sorts, but especially on an intellectual and artistic community blind to its own powerlessness even as it imperviously prescribes to its own the urgency of being both "affirmative and contestatory." This "crisis" in intellectual life can only be resolved and the high-tech world of "infotainment" be resisted if theorists face up to the powerful ubiquity of an economic genre "of which we are also a part." As if to rejoin Lévinas and Lyotard, Conley intimates that the inaugural situation of ethics is itself *already* situated within the economic situation that we associate today with postindustrial

capitalism, and whose basic exploitative mechanisms and effects have (as Lyotard has argued for many years) manifestly transcended the realm of the traditionally or strictly economical to pervade the "new" postmodern markets of aesthetics, sexuality, and knowledge, once the putative domains of nonquantitative
concerns.

   The difficulty of separating the ethical from the political, the economic from
the ethical, the political from the economical, is also addressed in the work of
Ernesto Laclau and Chantal Mouffe, especially *Hegemony and Socialist Strategy*, by their insistence on the primacy of the political as such over and beyond
any reified notions of class, economy, ethics, or community. For them, the current theoretical problem that most seriously needs to be addressed is not the capitalist production of new markets but the rise of "new social movements" (feminism, ecology, civil rights, gay rights, antinuclear) whose appearance and
impact on the contemporary political scene can no longer be registered simply in
terms of exploited labor power. Rejecting what they see as the essentialism of
classic Marxist theories of historical and economic determinism, they redefine
the Gramscian notion of hegemony as a specifically *political* logic that articulates
different social sectors or identities (what they call subject positions) into historical blocs that are less necessary than contingent. Insisting upon the early Al-
thusser's Lacanian conception of social relations as "overdetermined," that is,
of "the incomplete, open and politically negotiable character of every identity"
(*Hegemony*, 104), Laclau and Mouffe deny any ultimate suturing of the social
into a totality that can be grasped as such. Going further in this respect than either
Nancy or Lyotard in the latter's suspicion of abstract concepts of the social or
communal whole that would totalize and reduce the field of social differences,
Laclau and Mouffe categorically state, in one of their most infamous formula-
tions, that "'society' is impossible" (*Hegemony*, 114). This is because, for
them, the social is nothing but the articulation of different subject positions,
which consists, to cite the Lacanian language that is so often theirs, in "the construction of nodal points which partially fix meaning." Hegemony is thus to be
thought *not* in the mundane and negative sense of some kind of despotic oppression achieved by one group over all others but positively as a *partial and provisional* cathexis of social identities that binds together *some* of the "loose ends"
into an alignment that remains historically and politically contingent. What Laclau and Mouffe call the "deconstructive logic" of hegemony introduces "the
horizon of an impossible totality" into the social through the play of overdetermination between the dispersed subject positions it articulates even as it disal-
lows any one of them from consolidating itself into the separate and transcendent
position of a subject, such as in the traditional Marxist view of the proletariat as
revolutionary subject, as the uniquely empowered and solely legitimate agent of
social change. While Laclau and Mouffe do not, as some contend, go so far as
utterly to dispense with the class subject position of alienated labor, they do sit-

uate it, however, as only one among numerous other subject positions (typified in the new social movements of the late twentieth century) in search of hegemonic articulation. There is, nonetheless, a motivation for what would otherwise be an absolutely free-moving and thus ultimately undetermined theory of social interaction, namely what Laclau and Mouffe call "antagonism," by which they mean a conflict, not between preexisting identities, but between identities whose self-definitions are mutually undone and hence irresolvable within their current social formation. Antagonism is, as they say, the " 'experience' of the limit of the social," a "witness of the impossibility of a final suture," and thus it constitutes "the limits of society, the latter's impossibility of fully constituting itself" (*Hegemony*, 125). Whence, the urgency of rearticulating subject positions through relations of difference and equivalence into a new hegemonic formation, whose triumph in no way precludes the advent of new antagonisms (or even the persistence of old ones). The theoretical elaboration of the concept of hegemony, as carried out by Laclau and Mouffe, while recognizing that the progress of history can never be assured or assumed and that past gains can always be subverted (i.e., the revolution is a myth), also underscores the urgency of a creative political engagement whose horizon is that of a "radical and plural democracy," to be achieved not by the mechanical unfolding of a historical narrative, but through an endlessly critical vigilance.

Thus, while the conflictual situation of antagonism and the practice of hegemonic articulation echo Lyotard's invention of "new idioms" to phrase the incommunicable wrong felt in a differend, what one could call a post-Marxist differend can also be heard in the difference between Lyotard's nearly limitless extension of the economic, insistence upon the ethical, and suspicion of official politics, on the one hand, and Laclau and Mouffe's restriction (some would say scandalous elimination) of the economic, insistence upon the political, and suspicion of the discourse of ethics, on the other hand.

Chantal Mouffe brings the question of the relation between the ethical and the political to the fore in her discussion of the category of "citizen." These remarks are situated in the debate raging among contemporary political philosophers between those who, defending a "Kantian" liberalist view, argue for the priority of individual rights over any common good as well as for a theory of personal liberty "understood in a negative way as absence of coercion," and those "communitarian" proponents of a civic republicanism whose participatory ideal of citizenship is understood in terms of the advancement toward a "substantive idea of the common good" that is, in turn, the organizing principle behind the cohesion of the political community. While the former view, with its insistence on the split between public and private, has "reduced citizenship to a mere legal status" and thus de-emphasized the "ideas of public-spiritedness, civic activity, and political participation," its historic success in the last few centuries has also incontrovertibly contributed to the spread of democratic principles in ways that are unthinkable from the premodern perspective of "republican virtue." Rejecting the claim that these two positions are incompatible, Mouffe seeks to "reestablish the lost connection between ethics and politics. . . . We should not accept a false dichotomy between individual liberty and rights on one side versus civic activity and political community on the other. Our choice is not at all between an aggregate of individuals without common public concern and a premodern community organized around a single substantive idea of the common good. How to envisage the modern democratic political community outside this dichotomy is the crucial question." The alternative is to see citizenship "not as a legal status but as a form of identification, a type of political identity: something to be constructed, not empirically given." This should allow for a discourse about community that still implies an "ethico-political bond" without positing the existence of any single common good: "Antagonistic forces will never disappear, and politics is characterized by conflict and division. Forms of agreement can be reached, but they are always partial and provisional since consensus is by necessity based upon acts of exclusion." Incorporating "the psychoanalytic insight that all identities are forms of identification," Mouffe argues that the social agent or citizen must be conceived anew according to such a political understanding:

> [The citizen] is a common political identity of persons who might be engaged in many different purposive enterprises and with differing conceptions of the good, but who accept submission to the rules prescribed by the *respublica* in seeking their satisfactions and in performing their actions. What binds them together is their common recognition of a set of ethico-political values. In this case, citizenship is not just one identity among others — as in liberalism — or the dominant identity that overrides all others — as in civic republicanism. It is an articulating principle that affects the different subject positions of the social agent . . . while allowing for a plurality of specific allegiances and for the respect of individual liberty.

Such a view of citizenship is aligned with postmodern critiques of rationalism and universalism to the extent that it "rejects the idea of an abstract universalist definition of the public" and of its putative opposition to the "domain of the private seen as the realm of particularity and difference," an opposition whose adumbration has also served to identify "the private with the domestic and played an important role in the subordination of women." The "exercise of citizenship" thus "consists [not] in adopting a universal point of view, made equivalent to Reason and reserved for men" but in identifying with the "ethico-political principles of modern democracy." In terms of the "never-ending" "struggle for the deepening of the democratic revolution," such a radically democratic concept of citizenship means that "no sphere is immune" from "a concern with equality and liberty" and that "relations of domination can be challenged everywhere.'' It therefore also reconciles ''the ideal of rights and pluralism with the ideas of public-spiritedness and ethico-political concern.''

But if this notion of the citizen thus designates a possible nodal point in the constitution of a radical democratic hegemony, there still remains the question of how a particular felt antagonism may get articulated at the citizenly level through communal action, especially if the negativity that is antagonism also constitutes the very limit of community. To the extent that the limits of legitimate social or political change then become an issue, the question raised is, in classic terms, that of the difference between reform and revolution. Taking issue (as does Fynsk) with the ''liberal utopianism'' of Richard Rorty, Ernesto Laclau displaces the opposition, on the one hand, by categorically rejecting the ''foundationalist'' myth of a revolution that would claim the pristine ground of an impossibly total overturning of a whole society, and on the other hand, by espousing a concept of reform that does not exclude the role of violence. Deconstructing Rorty's liberalist opposition between (legitimate, democratic) persuasion and (illegitimate, undemocratic) force, Laclau argues that not only is persuasion a ''form of force'' but also that ''the existence of violence and antagonism is the very condition of a free society.'' This is because society is not, as in the ''revolutionary'' or foundationalist point of view, built upon some one focal point that can be founded anew but is ''pragmatically constructed from many starting points.'' The necessary antagonisms that ensue also describe the very limit and condition of the social in its radically democratic sense, the ''first paradox of a free community.'' As such, the theoretical problem of democratic politics is not the ''elimination of power'' as it is for a liberal like Rorty but the conceptualization of ''the forms of power that are compatible with democracy.'' Such a conceptualization is to be found in the theory of hegemony as the contingent articulation of political identities, for such an articulation does not exclude but rather grounds its own possibility in the very existence of antagonisms. Similarly, debates about the optimal relation between the public and the private need to be displaced in favor of a political discourse that stresses the necessity in a democratic society for there being *multiple* public spaces. Finally, the universalist values that underpin much liberalist thinking need less to be abandoned (or ''ironized,'' as Rorty would have it) than historicized in terms of their pragmatic necessity for the initial formation of democratic institutions. Such a historicist recasting will thus reveal the ''historicity of Being'' and ''the contingent character of universalist values'' in ways that should encourage human beings to see themselves less as the pawns of destiny than as the collective agents of their fate.

Commenting upon the work of both Laclau and Mouffe, Paul Smith challenges them to evolve a more positive version of the subject, lest the post-Marxist denial of strict determinism fall into quietism. By reference to the work of Alain Touraine, Smith returns to a privileging of the political understood as the ensemble of social processes captured in overdetermined relations. Notwithstanding the rejection of essentialism and totalization, Smith defends a notion of identity based upon a subject's particular capacities for action. This capacity Smith sees as consistent with the historicity of subject positions themselves, owing to his view that discourse is historical not just in its syntagmatic but in its paradigmatic relation as well. If some notion of agency is to be conceptualized, Smith argues for theorizing the subject's relation to the modern state and for retaining traditional concepts like party, class, and identity.

Also urging a return to traditional Marxist categories, notably the dialectic, is Richard Terdiman's argument presented here that the poststructuralist/postmodernist thought of Nancy and Lyotard, among others, militates delusionally against any and all forms of relationship and determination. Yet in its desire to free the play of textuality from all possible constraints, poststructuralism would not only fail to recognize its own counterdiscursive relation to the nineteenth-century metanarratives of Hegel and Marx as that *against which* it is written, but it also invents as problems precisely those categories dialectical thought had as its purpose to explain: history (as "diachronic and deterministic") and community (as "synchronic and deterministic"). Its radicalism thwarted by its absolute insistence on the absence of relation and determination, poststructuralism cannot therefore think history and community—which, concludes Terdiman, "however problematical, may be more thinkable than we thought."

While some may well disagree with Terdiman's characterization of poststructuralism as antirelational, his essay's signal merit is to bring into sharp relief the question of the *determination* of relation as the important theoretical question that imposes itself in the aftermath of Nancy's deconstruction of community as an essence immanent unto itself and his foregrounding of the *relation* of being together as foundational. And while, Terdiman notwithstanding, all of the contributors to this volume agree that community must be thought relationally, the kinds of relational logic they privilege and/or put to work are as varied and as numerous as the contributors themselves: dialectical, contingent, causal, overdetermined, structural, equivalential, hegemonic, differential, liminal, unconscious or libidinal, and so forth. To think community no longer as a foundational or immanent *com-unus* but as inaugurated and sustained in difference is thus no idle complication but a determined way to raise new questions and chart alternative possibilities about what it is for us to be together, about what it means for us to have in common above all the commonality of our difference.

The communitarian relation is not, however—as the contributors also all know—just something to be "thought" or theorized in the abstract; it is also what must be confronted and engaged as the concrete materiality within which "we" are all necessarily and always already inscribed. The fact that we are "we" (that is, part of some larger social unit) literally even before any of us can be said to be an "I" speaks to the exigency of thinking *from* the communal and not toward it as if it were a mere extension of the "I." But the shifting, dissonant, even conflictual "we" that has brought forth this volume knows that it too is no more than a ragged, indeterminate, but potentially illimited community at loose ends, whether that "we" be taken to refer to the conference's small organizing and editorial committee, its variably sized reading groups, its larger collectivity of colloquium participants and audience, or to the wider public of readers we hope our work will prompt to engage in further discussion of what our being-together can and should mean. Having thus grappled on the practical as well as the theoretical level with the necessity of dissonance in this collective project, we draw the crucial lesson, even as we write, that "we" always speaks with more than one voice. For even "I" who write this Introduction could not have done without the helpful ideas, suggestions, and, indeed, words of others (especially Peggy Kamuf, Steve Nimis, and Mitchell Greenberg, but also Britton Harwood, Marie-Claire Vallois, Peter Rose, Juliana Schiesari, Linda Singer, Verena Andermatt Conley, Tom Conley, and James Creech).

Though some may feel dismay at the lack of more specific attention to communities in which "they" as well as "we" may belong (women, men, blacks, browns, whites, immigrants, gays, intellectuals, etc.), the intervention "we" claim is precisely on and at a theoretical, even willfully abstract, level that is also (and necessarily) the fundamental as well as the practical one of "our" experience. *Community at Loose Ends* is thus not an answer to the question but a questioning of some contemporary "answers" that seeks to demarcate the parameters of a discussion this volume can only hope to set in motion.

Note

1. Portions published as *The Inoperative Community*, ed. Peter Connor, trans. Peter Connor, Lisa Garbus, Michael Holland, and Simona Sawhney (Minneapolis: University of Minnesota Press, 1991).

Of Being-in-Common

Jean-Luc Nancy

What could be more common than to be, than being? We are. Being, or existence, is what we share. When it comes to sharing nonexistence, we are not here. Nonexistence is not for sharing. But being is not a thing that we could possess in common. Being is in no way different from existence, which is singular each time. We shall say then that being is not common in the sense of a common property, but that it is in common. Being is in common. What could be simpler to establish? And yet, is there anything of which ontology has been more unaware up to now?

We are quite far from having reached the point where ontology would be directly available without any delay as something communal, where — according to the strict logic of its withdrawal and its difference — being would withdraw into the being-in-common of existing beings (and here I am bracketing the question of whether to extend "existence" to all beings or only to certain of them such as people, animals, and so forth). Henceforth the question should be the community of being, and not the being of community. Or if you prefer: the community of existence, and not the essence of community.

(Even so, it is not certain that the point of communitary ontology can be "reached" in the manner of a locatable stage in an incremental process of philosophical knowledge. The community of being is not merely some truth that has been unknown or rediscovered by an obstinately individualist, solipsistic, or monadic tradition. It is likely that the experience of this community is also buried in this whole tradition, and that for reasons that are surely fundamental, it is accessible only to a praxis whose "theoretical" burial is, in a manner of speaking,

1

constitutive. In a certain vocabulary, one could say that the experience of being-in-common is no doubt more self-evident and even more remote, even more "thoughtless" than the Cartesian experience of existence—an experience and a self-evidence that for Descartes are already *common*. But this "thoughtlessness," as a praxis, has all the power of permanent subversion or revolution that constitute what we call "thought." But be that as it may, today I am only proposing to discern the preliminary conditions for accepting "thought" in this sense.)

In imitation of a statement of Kant's thesis on being, one could say: *Community is not a predicate of being or of existence. One changes nothing in the concept of existence by adding or subtracting communitary character. Community is simply the real position of existence.*

No doubt this imitation has pedagogical virtue. It should give us to understand that being-in-common, or being-with, cannot be added in a secondary and extrinsic way to being-oneself or being-in-solitude. Such an imitation should even give us to understand that Heidegger's *Mitsein*, and even his *Mit-da-sein*, is not thought out as radically or as decisively as it should be. It would really need to be understood that the "mit" does not modify the "sein" (as if being could already sustain itself in some way, as if being *were itself*; that is, as if being *were* or *existed* absolutely); and it would need to be understood that the "mit" does not even qualify the "Dasein," but that it constitutes it essentially. In a baroque German, I would point to a "*seindamit*," or to the "with" as itself a modality, both exclusive and originary of "being-there" or of being-the-there.

But such an imitation of Kant immediately betrays its impropriety. For existence, conceived as a predicate, was supposed to link up with the concept of a thing (which Kant denies). Yet, by virtue of Kant's thesis, existence itself is neither a concept nor a thing. Kant calls it a limit thesis. (And Kant's thesis, once transformed, gives us Heidegger's thesis on the ontological difference, which is itself a limit-thesis for any ontological thesis.) Existence is "the simple position" of the thing. Being is neither substance nor cause of the thing; rather, it is a being-the-thing in which the verb "to be" has a transitive value of a "positioning," but one in which the "positioning" is based on nothing else but (and because of nothing else) than on (and because of) *Dasein*, being-there, being thrown down, given over, abandoned, offered up by existence. (The *there* is not a grounding for existence, but rather its taking *place*, its arrival, its coming—which also means its difference, its withdrawal, its excess, its "exscription.")

In saying that community is the position of existence, we are saying that community is the position of the position. Indeed it is. We are saying that community is the decisive mode of the positing of position (and consequently, of being). How can that be understood?

That means: In existence and as existence, position (Kant's *Setzung* as distinct from his notion of *Position*) never posits *an* instance of existence as *a* distinct thing, independent, related to the unity and unicity of its essence. It is a matter of existence and not of essence. Existence is the essence, if you like, but insofar as it is posited. In the positing, essence is offered or given. That is, essence is exposed to being, or to existing, outside of being as a simple subsistence, or as an immanence.

In immanent subsistence, there is no *self*—in French, no *soi*. There is an essence, with its predicates, but no *self*, no *soi* of that essence or for that essence. If one is rigorous about it, one can not even say that it is "present to itself." Or else, this presence is such that it becomes confused with the night of an absence where nothing can be distinguished.

In the position, that is—you are no doubt ahead of me—in the *ex*-position, in the being-abandoned-to-the-world, essence is exposed. To what is it exposed? To nothing other than itself. This could be formulated in a very Hegelian way. For that matter, the sole task for an ontology of community is, *through* thinking about being and its *différance*, to radicalize or to aggravate Hegelian thinking about the Self until it caves in. But as I was saying, this could be formulated in a very Hegelian way, namely, that essence is exposed to being *of* itself, *for* itself, and *unto* itself what it is *in* itself. (This is basically what Heidegger talks about in his thesis on the *Jemeinigkeit* of existence, but this enunciation has the drawback of veiling the Self under the Ego. It leads to the ambiguity of appropriations that are individual, subjective, and unilateral, despite the related theme of the *Mitsein*, which for this reason must also be radicalized.)

The Self to which existence exposes is not a property subsisting before that exposition and which then would be mediated dialectically. The reason is simply that there is not "Self." (Grammatically speaking, *Self*—as in the French *soi*—is an object exactly like the reflexive pronoun *se* with which it forms a pair, and exactly like the French word for "others," *autrui*, which, as Lévinas has pointed out, also has this particularity of being an "objective case.") "Soi" has no nominative case, but is always declined. It is always the object or the complement of an action, an address, or an attribution. "Soi" is always only to "soi," of "soi," for "soi," and so forth. And whatever paradox we must see in this, "soi" is not *subject*. To be *to* "soi," and not to *be* "soi," is the condition of the being of existence, as exposition. Stated another way, "soi" is being in the objective case, and there is no other *case* of being. That's where it *falls* (*cadere*, *casus*), that is its essential accident (*accidere*), or it is the accident of essence insofar as essence *is*, and does not subsist. "Soi" is the arrival, the coming, the event of being.

Thus we will have to say that in itself—*en soi*—essence is not subsistence and property, but rather being *unto* itself, being exposed to the declension of existing. Essence is in itself existence. In the final analysis that is the meaning of Heidegger's axiom that existence is the essence of the *Dasein*. I have had occasion to transcribe that by saying existence is without essence. Although that's probably a handy formula, it is more correct and precise—and also more difficult—to say that the essence of essence is existence. Meanwhile, to prevent this new essence from becoming a superessence, a foundation or a substance, we will have to make clear that the verb "is" in this formulation must take on the transitive value that Heidegger is attempting to give as its true value in *Was ist das, die Philosophie?* A "true value," moreover, that cannot be semanticized, a transitive sense that transpierces all "sense." *All* ontology is reduced to the transitivity of being.

Essence exposes *itself*—*s*'expose—essentially to existence. It exposes "soi" to being-unto-itself. The "unto-itself" defines the boundary, the limit or the fold of declension where "soi" is "on its own," *other before* any assignment of same and other. (I could speak of it in terms of "relation," except that "relation" is still too exterior for something which does not allow separation of interiors from exteriors.) Despite what Hegel maintained, "soi" is not just the "soi" of self-consciousness needing to be recognized in order to recognize it*self*. Nor is it merely, as Lévinas claims, hostage to others. It is "in itself" an objective case, the other of its declension. "Being-self" is being-unto itself, being-exposed-to-itself; but "soi" in itself *is nothing but the exposition*. Being-unto-itself is being-unto-exposition. It is being-unto-others, if "others" declines "in itself and for itself" the declension of "soi." All ontology can be reduced to this being-unto-self-unto-others. Transitively, essence *is* nothing more than the exposition of its subsistence: the exposed face of what subsists, existing only insofar as it is exposed, forever unavailable and beyond appropriation for the interior of subsistence and for its thick, opaque, unexposed, immanent—in a word: inaccessible—for its inexistent center.

The unexposable (or the unpresentable) is the inexistent. On the contrary, existence is only the presence to "self" in which the "to" declines, differentiates, and essentially alters the "self" for *being*, which is to say, for *existing*, which is to say, for *exposing*. The becoming-self "of" the self is a becoming-imperceptible, as Deleuze might say: imperceptible to any assignment of essence. Becoming-self is the undefined extension of the surface where substance is exposed. For that reason it is a becoming-other which includes no mediation of the same and the other. There is no alchemy of subjects. There is an extensive/intensive dynamic of the surfaces of exposition. These surfaces are the limits upon which the self declines *itself*. They partition and share being and existence.

This is what we will transcribe by saying that there is no communion, there is no common being, but there is being *in* common. Once ontology becomes this logic of being in itself as being *to* itself, all ontology can be reduced to the in-common of the *unto*-itself. This "reduction," or this total reevaluation, or this revolution of ontology, though dimly perceived, is probably what has been happening to us since Hegel and Marx, since Heidegger and Bataille. The meaning of being is not common, and yet the *in*-common of being transpierces all meaning. To put it in another way: existence *is* only in being partitioned and shared. But this partition, which we could call the "unto-itselfness" of existence, does not distribute a substance or a common meaning. It parcels out only the exposition of being, the declension of self, the faceless trembling of exposed identity: *we* are what it divides and parcels out.

At its limit, philosophy thus has to do with this: that sense does not coincide with being. Or, in a more difficult and demanding way, we could say that the sense of being is not to be found in a coincidence of being with itself (at least for as long as being is presumed to be the place of sense, and of a sense that is presentable in the ideal identity of a self-constituting signification, a privileged example of which would be in community, or in the common sense of common being). Philosophy thus has to do with the limit where community is also suspended. There is no self-communication of sense, and community perhaps has nothing, or above all is nothing common. Above all it does not even have any co-humanity and no longer any co-naturality or co-presence with whatever there may be of a world that community makes uninhabitable for itself to the degree that it invests it. At its limits—those of community, of philosophy—the world is not a *world,* it is a heap, and perhaps a foul one (*un monde immonde*).

This is where we are now, that is what makes our *era,* an era which can only think itself, in sum, as a limit to an era, if it is true that an "era" is a form or an aspect of the "world." Significations are suspended. We can no longer say, "Here is sense, here is co-humanity, and here is its philosophy—or here are its philosophies, in their fertile competition." And the gesture of philosophy offers itself nakedly and emptily, as if to be reinvented. Not reinvented in order to discover other significations, but henceforth to be only on the limit. Philosophy offers itself as a gesture toward the sense of sense, a gesture toward an unheard-of exteriority beyond appropriation. (The only thing we know is that sense cannot appropriate to itself the real, it cannot appropriate existence. It is not the meaningful self-constitution of the essence of the real.) Such is the "sense" of all the major "themes" of contemporary thought, whether one is speaking of "being," of "language," of "the other," "singularity," "writing," "mimesis, "multiplicities," "the event," "the body," or many others still. In so many forms, forms that are not necessarily compatible, it is always a question of what we could call, in the traditional lexicon of doctrines, a realism of unappropriable truth. Which above all does not mean "of absent truth."

But in what way would truth be henceforth "present," or would it come to presence, if the constitution of a common sense and of the common-being of sense is abandoned at its limits?

Community, perhaps, must give us a few indications. Or more exactly, it is the "end" of any attempt to appropriate the sense of community, which ought to give us indications (the end of attempts to appropriate "love," "family," "state," "communion," the "people," and so on). At this end point, this limit where we are, there remains in spite of everything—and it shows therefore—that *we* are there. The era of the limit abandons us together on the limit, for if not, it would not be an "era" or a "limit," and "we" would not be there. If we suppose that there was before (or elsewhere) something else, we can say that there remains this remainder of community that we are *in* common, within—or faced with— the disconnection of common sense. At least we are with one another, or together. Although that appears de facto obvious, we can pass no law in its favor (we can link it to no essence of co-humanity), but it persists and resists, de facto, in a kind of material insignificance. Can we, on the limit, try to decipher this in-significance?

We are *in* common, *with* one another. What do this "in" and this "with" mean? (Or to put it another way, what does "we" mean, what is the meaning of this pronoun which, in one way or another, must be inscribed in any discourse?)

It is not only, it is not so much, the question of *a* sense, but it is rather a question of the place, the space-time, the mode, the system of signification in general, if by definition sense communicates, communicates itself and causes communication. And that is why this deciphering can no longer be simply philosophical. That is why it can only take place at the end of philosophy—and of all logic, grammar, and literature in general. "We": first-person plural. Let us try to represent to one another the difficulty of this simple designation. "With," "together," or "in common" obviously do not mean "in one another," nor do they mean "in each other's place." That would imply an exteriority. (Even in love, one is "in" the other only outside the other. The child "in" its mother is also exterior in that interiority, although in quite another way. And in the most assembled crowd, one is not in the place of the other.) But "with" does not mean "next to," or "juxtaposed," either. The logic of the "with"—of the being-with, of the *Mitsein* that Heidegger makes contemporary and correlative with the *Dasein*—is the singular logic of an inside-outside. It is perhaps the very logic of singularity in general. And it would thus be the logic of what belongs neither to the pure inside nor to the pure outside. (Inside and outside in fact merge. To be purely outside, outside of everything [ab-solute], would mean to be purely in it- self, apart from itself, to itself, *without even* having the possibility of distinguish- ing itself as "itself.") A logic of the limit pertains to what is between two or several, belonging to all and to none—not belonging to itself, either.

(It is not certain that this logic is restricted to man, nor even to living beings. Would not stones, mountains, the bodies of a galaxy be "together" seen from a certain perspective not ours? It is a question that we will leave here without an answer, the question of the community of the world.)

To begin with, the logic of being-with corresponds to nothing other than what we could call the banal phenomenology of unorganized groups of people. Passengers in the same train compartment are simply seated next to each other in an accidental, arbitrary, and completely exterior manner. They are not linked. But they are also quite together inasmuch as they are travelers on this train, in this same space and for this same period of time. They are between the disintegration of the "crowd" and the aggregation of the group, both extremes remaining possible, virtual, and near at every moment. This suspension is what makes "being-with": a relation without relation, or rather, being exposed simultaneously to relationship and to absence of relationship. Such an exposure is made up of the simultaneous immanence of the retreat and the coming of the relation, and it can be decided at any moment by the least incident—or more probably, and more secretly, it never ceases being decided at each instant—in one direction or in the other, in one direction *and* in the other, in "freedom" and in "necessity," in "consciousness" and in "unconsciousness," the undecided decision of stranger and neighbor, of solitude and collectivity, of attraction and repulsion.

This exposure to relation/nonrelation is nothing other than the exposure of singularities to each other. (I say "singularities" because these are not only individuals that are at stake, as a facile description would lead one to believe. Entire collectivities, groups, powers, and discourses are exposed here, "within" each individual as well as among them. "Singularity" would designate precisely that which, each time, forms a point of exposure, traces an intersection of limits on which there is exposure.) To be exposed is to be on the limit where, at the same time, there is both inside and outside, and neither inside nor outside. It is not yet even to be "face to face." It is anterior to entrapment by the stare that captures its prey or takes its hostage. Exposure comes before any identification, and singularity is not an identity. It is exposure itself, its punctual actuality. (But identity, whether individual or collective, is not a sum total of singularities; it is itself a singularity.) It is to be "in oneself" according to a partition of "self" (meaning both a division and a distribution), it is constitutive of "self," a generalized ectopia of all "proper" places (such as intimacy, identity, individuality, name), places that are what they are only by virtue of being exposed on their limits, by their limits, and as these very limits. That does not mean that there is nothing "proper" to these places, but that the proper would be brought about essentially by a "cleaving" or by a "schism." Which means that the proper is without essence, and yet, is exposed.

Can there be any other mode of being other than one in which *being* is never "being," but is always modalized in the exposing? This mode of being, of existing—without presupposing that there is exposition (which is what "exposition" means in the first place), does presuppose that there is no common being, no substance, no essence, or common identity, but that there is being *in* common. If relation must be posed between two terms already provided, between two given existences, the *in* (the *with*, the Latin *cum* of "community") does not designate any mode of the relation. It would designate rather a being *insofar as it is* relation, identical to existence itself—that is, identical to the arrival of existence, to existence. And yet, neither the term "being" nor the term "relation" names that adequately, even when they are placed in this relationship of equivalence, because here there is not an equivalence of terms, which would once again make a relation exterior to "being" and to "relation." Instead we will have to settle for the formulation that being is *in* common, without ever being common.

Nothing is more common than being: it is the self-evidence of existence. Nothing is more uncommon than being: it is the self-evidence of community. Both the one and the other reveal the self-evidence of thought without being philosophies of revelation. For each divides and shares the other, denying it its self-evidence. Being, by itself, is not its own evidence of itself. It is not equal to itself nor to its meaning. That's what existence is, that's what community is, and that's what exposes them. Each is the bringing into play of the other. The *in* play of the *in* common: what gives play, and birth, to thought, even to the "play" of these words in which, in reality, nothing less than *our* communication is exposed (a communication that is itself exposed to the lack of commonality, to the absence of "common measure" between language and the translucidness that we are presuming in a "communication" that would be communicating *a* supposed common sense instead of communicating the sense of "us").

The in-play of the in-common. To think that, without respite, is "philosophy," or what is left of it at its end, if it remains communal; that is politics, that is art, or what remains of it that is walking in the street, that is crossing borders, that is celebration and mourning; that is to be hard at it, or sitting in a train compartment; that is knowing how capital capitalizes the common and dissolves the *in* (of *in* common); that is always to ask what "revolution" means, what revolution wants to experience; that is resistance, that is existence.

Being "is" the *in* that divides and joins at the same time, that "partitions and shares," the limit where partitioning and sharing are exposed. (We should say: being is in the "in," inside of what has no inside.) The limit is nothing: it is nothing but this extreme *abandonment* in which all property, all singular instance of property, in order to be what it is, is first of all given over to the outside (but not to the outside of an inside . . .). Can we think this abandon in which the *propre* happens, being first—that is to say from the start, beginning at the edge, from the border of its property—being first received, perceived, felt, touched, handled, desired, rejected, called up, named, communicated? In truth, this abandon is very much anterior to birth, or else it is nothing else but birth itself, the infinite birth unto the death that finishes it by achieving abandonment. And this abandonment abandons to nothing else but being-in-common, that is not to say, to *particular* communication or to *particular* community—as if they were instances of reception or of recording. But abandonment itself "communicates"; it communicates singularity to itself by an infinite "outside," *as* this infinite "outside." It makes the *propre* happen (person, group, assembly, society, people, and so on) by exposing it. This advent is what Heidegger called *Ereignis*, that is, "propriation," but also and from the start, "event." Event is not the event that takes place, but the coming of a place, of a space-time as such, the tracing of its limit, its exposure.

Can this exposition be exposed? Can it be presented or represented? (And what concept fits here? Is it a matter of representing, of signifying, of staging or gaming?) Can we present the sense of the *in*-common through which only sense in general is possible?

If we do so, if we assign and show the being (or the essence) of the *in*-common, and if as a consequence we present community to itself (in a people, a State, a mind, a destiny, a work), sense thus (re)presented immediately undoes the whole exposition and with it, the sense of sense itself. But if we do not do it, if the exposition itself remains unexposed, which means in fact that we represent that there is nothing to present of the *in*-common except the repetition of a "human condition" that does not even attain a "co-humanity" (a flat condition that is neither human nor inhuman), then the sense of the sense crumbles as well. Everything tips over into a juxtaposition without relationships and without singularities. The identity of the one or the identity of the multiple (of nonidentity) are identical, and do not affect the plural exposition of the *in*, do not affect *our* exposure.

Whatever we do, however, or whatever we don't do, nothing takes place, nothing truly takes place but this exposition. Its necessity is the very opening of what, because we cannot linger over these words here, I will call liberty, equality, justice, fraternity. Even so, if nothing takes place but this exposure—that is to say, if being *in* common resists communion and disaggregation invincibly—this exposition and this resistance are neither immediate nor immanent. They are not a given that could be affirmed by merely picking it up. It is certain that being-in-common insists and resists, otherwise I would not even have written this and you would never have read it. But that does not entail the conclusion that all we have to do is to say it to expose it. The necessity of being-in-common is not that of a physical law, and whoever wants to expose it must also expose himself (that is what we can call "thought," "writing," *and* their partition and sharing). On the contrary, the complacency that threatens any discourse of community (mine too, therefore) is this: to think that one is (re)presenting, by one's own communication, a co-humanity whose truth, however, is not a given and (re)presentable essence.

What is given, what is signified today is much more on the order of a tirelessly dialecticized identity of identity and nonidentity (one/multiple, individual/

collective, conscious/unconscious, will/material forces, ethics/economics, and so forth). That is perhaps what we are including under the heading "technics": the co-humanity of an an-humanity, a community of operations, not of existences. "Technics" could just as likely be the completed form of a reciprocal constitution of being and sense, as it could the hyperbolic form of their infinite disjunction. That may be what has made possible the recurrent and invariable alternation of valorizations and devalorizations of this same "technics" for so many centuries. But that may be the very thing—not what is happening in satellites or in fiber optics, but what we think of confusedly as "technics"—that the "given" is hiding from us even as it persists in being *offered up* as the *in*. We do not seize control, we do not appropriate what is offered up. Or rather, in the very appropriation that accepts and that receives the offering, one remains exposed to the suspense (and to the freedom) of the offering, and to what is not appropriable in it.

Henceforth, then, there may well be a task that is indissociably and perhaps even indiscernibly "philosophical" and "communitary" (a task for thought and politics, if these words fit without further examination), and that task would be to expose the unexposable *in*. To *expose* it, which is to say, in presenting or representing it, to make the (re)presentation itself, in turn, the site and the focus of an exposition; so that thought itself might risk itself and abandon itself to "community," and "community" to "thought." That might immediately conjure up the figure of a "thinking community," of Rabelais's Abbaye de Thélème or of a romantic literary society fancying itself a republic (a republic of kings), or something like a "literary communism." (I recently used that expression; its equivocal character makes me reject it now. I am not speaking here of a community of letters. . . .) But it is not a question of everyone being a philosopher (as Marx hoped at one point), no more than it is a question of having philosophy "reign" (as Plato wanted). Or else, it is a matter of one and the other at the same time, of one against the other (then it becomes thinking on the limit, where we don't know what the word "philosophy" designates); but what is at stake here is not to provide sense, nor even to pose the question as a question of being: What *is* the sense? What sense does being have, is it being-in-common? What is called into play here, not opposite to, but decidedly other than the question of sense, is exposing ourselves to the partition and sharing of the *in*, to this distribution of "sense" that first *withdraws* being from sense and sense from being—or else, does not identify one with the other, and each as such, except through the *in* of the "common," through a "with" of sense that properly disappropriates it.

    Not that I "have" sense, or some quantity of sense, but that I have a part *in* sense and I am in it in the exclusive mode of being-in-common. I am an *ego sum, ego existo* that would be actual only in exposing partition and sharing, distribution of this existing being, as its most intimate self-evidence. (But already self-evidence is posited by Descartes himself as common evidence, shared by each and every one before any accession to the status of evidence and evidential thought, or rather, as having in this very sharing the obscure threshold of its self-evidence.)

I have a part *in it*: existence takes place exposed on this in, to *this in*. Inseparable, therefore, from a *we exist*. And more than inseparable: having its provenance in an enunciation *in* common where (rather than any subject determinable according to the concepts of philosophy) the *in* speaks and is spoken — presence coming to itself insofar as it is the limit and the partition/sharing of presence. Something that is exposing and inexposable which, nevertheless, *we* expose in common.

It will be tempting to say, "Here we have a description of the status quo, if not of all social and political arrangement, at least of democracy." (Or else, and in a more cunning manner, one will be tempted to say that it is a description of a kind of democratic noumenon entrenched behind any sociopolitical phenomenon.) It is nothing of the kind. Whatever is not democracy either exposes nothing (tyranny, dictatorship) or presents an essence of being and of common meaning (totalitarian immanence). But democracy, for its part, exposes only that such an essence is inexposable. There can be no doubt that it is the lesser evil. However, the *in*-common, the *with*, withdraws its pretensions: from inappropriable exposition (no doubt enigmatically volunteered between the lines of the *Social Contract* despite Rousseau) we pass to the spectacle of general appropriation, through the logic of the inexposable and against it at the same time. (The word "spectacle" will have to do here to indicate an inside-out, appropriated, controlled exposition, what the situationists must have been trying to get at using the same word. As for general appropriation, clearly it cannot be general except by being immediately particular and privative.) Appropriation of capital, of the individual, of production and reproduction (of the "technic") inasmuch as it is "in-common," taking the place of the taking-place of the in-common. Democracy, therefore, lacks being — not a representation of the in-common (as if it were an exterior operation), but an exposition of it; that is, it doesn't quite expose itself in it, or expose *us* in it, or expose us to "our*selves*."

History — a history that is not even "part of history" but is always our present interest — has taught us the risks that are linked to a critique of democracy (risks no less grave than extermination, pure expropriation, and boundless exploitation). Therefore, the task is no doubt to displace the idea of "critique" itself. But history also teaches us the risk of what we always call "democracy": settling for violent and flat appropriation of the *in* of being-in-common, an appropriation that is not even identifiable (unless once again we identify it as "technics" — a bit like when we speak of "technical measures"). The risk of deserting the breach of the *in*. "Philosophy" and "community" have this in common: a categorical imperative, anterior to all morality (but politically without ambiguity, for politics in this sense precedes all morality, instead of succeeding it or accommodating it), a categorical imperative not to let go of sense *in* common.

Translated by James Creech

On the Limit

Peggy Kamuf

Nothing can authorize anyone—me, for example—more than anyone else to respond to the text by Jean-Luc Nancy, "Of Being-in-Common."* Indeed, not having been trained as a philosopher, I should be less authorized to respond in this place where perhaps ultimate demands are being made on the possibilities of philosophical discourse. Yet, if the ultimate demand of thought is to think together not what or who we are, but only *that* we are in common without commonality, then indeed, as Nancy writes, the task "can no longer be simply philosophical." I will proceed, then, in the hope that my not-yet-philosophical thinking may somewhere cross this no-longer-simply-philosophical thinking whose necessity Nancy discerns and whose possibility is opened up by his writing.

For a few years now, I have been following Nancy's development of this thinking of being-in-common—with *Le Partage des voix* (1982), *L'Impératif catégorique* (1983), *La Communauté désoeuvrée* (1986), and most recently, most powerfully perhaps, *L'Expérience de la liberté* (1988). It was thus with a certain number of *renvois* to these other works that I could come to read the essay "Of Being-in-Common." I would like to get into my response via one such *renvoi*, which comes from *La Communauté désoeuvrée*:

> Because there is this unfinishing [*désoeuvrement*] that partitions our
> being in common, there is "literature," that indefinitely repeated and

---

*This essay was read at a discussion of Nancy's text with the Critical Studies and the Human Sciences Research group of UCLA in November 1988.

suspended gesture of touching the limit, indicating and inscribing it but
without crossing it or abolishing it in the fiction of a common body. To
write for others means in reality to write because of others. The writer
gives nothing and destines nothing to others; the project s/he has in
view is not to communicate anything whatsoever, neither a message nor
her/himself. To be sure, there are always messages and persons, and it
is important that both (treating them, if I can, as identical for the
moment) be communicated. But writing is the gesture which obeys the
sole necessity of exposing the limit—not the limit of communication,
but the limit on which communication takes place. (167; my translation)

This passage finds echoes with those moments of the essay that I found most
compelling—that is, most demanding of response. These are the moments when
the text we are reading partially folds back over itself and bids us to suspend our
expectant watch for a message that will close off the communicative relay, that
will signal that the communication is at an end and has reached its end, its des-
tination.

Nancy writes: "The writer gives nothing and destines nothing to others; the
project s/he has in view is not to communicate anything whatsoever, neither a
message nor her/himself." The echo with "Of Being-in-Common" might be
heard in a passage like the one beginning on page 19, for example, where Nancy
asks: "Can this exposition be exposed? Can it be presented or represented? . . .
Can we present the sense of the *in*-common through which only sense in general
is possible?" To these questions about the possibility of presenting or representing exposition (and this may be as good a place as any to recall that all these
words—presentation, representation, exposition, communication—are so many
names we also give to what is going on here and now, in the space of writing/
reading/hearing/speaking in common), Nancy first responds with the two versions of a certain failing or falling of exposition that present themselves: Either
"we assign and show the being (or the essence) of the *in*-common, and . . . as a
consequence we present community to itself," in which case "sense thus (re)-
presented immediately undoes the whole exposition and with it, the sense of
sense itself"; or else, we do not present or represent it, "which means in fact that
we represent that there is nothing to present of the *in*-common except the repetition of a 'human condition' that does not even attain a 'co-humanity,'" in
which case once again "the sense of the sense crumbles."

You will have already heard the folding over or folding back of this questioning on itself. That is, the question: "Can this exposition be exposed" asks to be
heard in at least two registers or two modes at once: On the one hand, can the
exposition I am talking about or thematizing—that of being-exposed-to-itself-in-
itself-and-thus-to-others—find an adequate representation, a name, an exposure
(as one says of a photographic exposure, a snapshot, in French a *cliché*)? On the

other hand, but also at the same time, can *this* exposition—by which I am attempting but necessarily failing to name being-in-common—be exposed at the limit of its failing to name, of its falling back into clichés (a "co-humanity" that Nancy notes parenthetically is "a flat condition . . . neither human nor inhuman"), and thus in effect already *displace* or ex-pose its own terms by those of others for whom, which is to say *because* of whom, I write?

These two modes or two registers—which I have just separated but which are in fact always articulated with each other—can be heard insisting together and equally whenever Nancy writes "*on* the limit," "*sur* la limite," which, I maintain, is what he is always doing even if the phrase itself occurs only once or twice in "Of Being-in-Common" (it occurs more frequently in *La Communauté désoeuvrée*). We commonly use the expression "to write on something," by which we understand: on a thesis, a theme, an object for discourse—here, for example, "being-in-common." But this is not just any theme or thesis; it is the very possibility of any sense at all taking place and taking place in the only place it can: on the limit. Thus, the prepositional phrase "on the limit" is topical not only because it announces a topic, but because it situates this writing on the limit on the limit. As Nancy says in the passage I have already read: "Writing is the gesture which obeys the sole necessity of exposing the limit—not the limit of communication, *but the limit on which communication takes place.*"

But we cannot assimilate this writing on the limit too quickly to our ordinary understanding of writing on *something*. "The limit," writes Nancy, "is nothing: it is nothing but this extreme *abandonment* in which all property, all singular instance of property, in order to be what it is, is first of all given over to the outside" (p. 8). In a sense, I will have done nothing here but repeat, reflect, recite that nothing—if that makes any sense. It is nothing, it is not a place, most of all it is not a dividing line between some inside and outside, yet it limits, and by limiting it also allows communication to happen, to take place. It is the limitation without which there is no possibility of sense, the restriction or constriction that at the same time opens up the possibility of sense, of proper meaning, proper place—of "le propre."

Nancy retains this designation—*le propre*—in the face of what would seem to be overwhelming reasons to abandon it; that is, he retains it to designate that which is first of all abandoned or "given over to the outside." For example, in another passage we read:

> To be exposed is to be on the limit where, at the same time, there is
> both inside and outside, and neither inside nor outside. . . . It is to be
> "in oneself" according to a partition [*partage*] of "self," . . . it is
> constitutive of "self," a generalized ectopia of all "proper" places
> (such as intimacy, identity, individuality, name), places that are what
> they are only by virtue of being exposed on their limits, by their limits,
> and as these very limits. *That does not mean that there is nothing*

"proper" *to these places, but that the proper would be brought about*
essentially by a "cleaving" or by a "schism." [Italics added.] Which
means that the proper *is* without essence, and yet, is exposed. (7)

One of the most productively disconcerting gestures sketched out here is this
refusal to abandon "le propre" even as the necessity of its self-abandonment is
being exposed. I would like to understand this gesture as a translation of the task
that Nancy ascribes earlier (3) to "an ontology of community," the task, therefore, that he has in some measure assumed. He writes: "The sole task for an
ontology of community is, *through* thinking about being and its *différance*, to
radicalize or aggravate Hegelian thinking about the Self until it caves in." The
key to this aggravation (in the strong sense of the word) would have to be the
displacement (the "generalized ectopia") of appropriation by and through exposition. The gesture of philosophy—of thought, of writing—or its task must
henceforth be toward "an unheard-of exteriority beyond appropriation." Beyond
appropriation, but not beyond the exposition of "le propre" to the outside that it
can neither appropriate nor exclude, that is thus not in any simple sense an outside. An ontology of community—of that which ontology has seemed to have
been altogether unaware up to now (1)—would entail a general displacement or
replacement of the verb "to be" (which has meant—"up to now"—to be appropriated) with its unappropriable other sense: to be exposed. (Here, I was
reminded of just such a radical aggravation of Hegelian thinking, Jacques
Derrida's *Glas*, in which he proposes at one point to replace the verb *être* by
the verb *bander*.) "Le propre" is exposed, and we cannot write, utter, or otherwise repeat that syntagma (which in one sense is all I am doing here) without
wrenching "le propre" out of reach of all appropriation. Its concept caves in,
indeed its collapse has already occurred before we can utter its name, but also *so*
that we can utter its name: the proper name and the name of the proper is always
in memoriam.

But I suspended the movement that follows from the question I cited earlier,
"Can this exposition be exposed?" It does not receive only negative answers that
describe an alternative between two modes of failing or falling before the task of
exposition. Nancy continues:

Whatever we do, however, or whatever we don't do, nothing takes
place, nothing truly takes place but this exposition. Its necessity is the
very opening of what, because we cannot linger over these words here,
I will call liberty, equality, justice, fraternity. [Elsewhere, in
L'Expérience de la liberté, it is precisely over these words that Nancy
lingers, so to speak.] Even so, if nothing takes place but this
exposure—that is to say, if being *in* common resists communion and
disaggregation invincibly—this exposition and this resistance are neither
immediate nor immanent. They are not a given that could be affirmed

by merely picking it up. It is certain that being-in-common insists and resists, *otherwise I would not even have written this and you would never have read it*. [Italics added.] But that does not entail the conclusion that all we have to do is to say it to expose it. The necessity of being-in-common is not that of a physical law, and whoever wants to expose it must also expose himself (that is what we can call "thought," "writing," *and* their partition and sharing [*partage*]). (9)

(Here I might ask parenthetically: What can possibly justify these long quotations from a text we have read in common? Why impose the repetition of this reading aloud from what we have each read in silence? What can this addition of a voice, and another language—for we must not forget that "Of Being-in-Common" exposes itself here to translation into another tongue—possibly add to what has already offered itself to our common understanding? I leave these questions suspended on the limit.) The exposition, neither immediate nor immanent, not appropriable therefore as a concept, takes place and is all that takes place: but that apparently limiting proposition ("nothing truly takes place but this exposition") is deceptive if we hear it only in the mode of a limitation. The phrase "the exposition takes place" translates as the taking place of the place. A place is thus also *given* ("the writer *gives* nothing . . ."), rather than taken away or reserved inaccessibly behind some barrier-limit. It is the place given to thought, to writing, to communication, and the place they give themselves through their *partage*. When Nancy writes: "It is certain that being-in-common insists and resists, otherwise I would not even have written this and you would never have read it," we are given to think that which insists and resists, that which impels, compels, or repels thinking, which has its place also here, between writing and reading, or rather within them both—one within the other according to an unrepresentable topology of the *in*-common. "Whoever wants to expose it must also expose himself": A self exposed: once again "le propre" is in play, takes place, can only take place with "it," in it, as being-in-common. With this co-exposition of "himself," Nancy has in mind a task for philosophy or for an ontology of community (he says "whoever wants to expose it *must* expose himself" and this necessity for thought can only be assumed as its task—a word he has elsewhere distinguished from *oeuvre*). This is specified a little further on:

Henceforth, then, there may well be a task that is indissociably and perhaps even indiscernibly "philosophical" and "communitary" (a task for thought and politics, if these words fit without further examination), and that task would be to expose the unexposable *in*. To *expose* it, which is to say, in presenting or representing it, to make the (re)presentation itself, in turn, the site and the focus of an exposition; so that thought itself might risk itself and abandon itself to "community," and "community" to "thought." (10)

The question I want to ask would be the following: Does this task of co-exposition, or self-exposition, comprise or define the task mentioned in the final paragraph: the task of displacing "the idea of 'critique' "? It is mentioned in a passage that evokes both the "risks that are linked to a critique of democracy," and, on the other hand, "the risk of what we still call 'democracy.' " The displacement of the idea of "critique" is situated between these opposed, but not symmetrical or commensurable, risks. It seems to me that the displacement in question must concern not just the idea of critique, but the idea of democracy, of what we always or still call democracy. Unless "critique" and "democracy" are or can be displaced names for each other? To negotiate between the parallel but asymmetrical risks requires, does it not, something like a self-exposition or self-critique of democracy—that is, an exposition of democracy at the limits of its concept, perhaps the exposition of the limits of the democratic concept as it has always been thought too uncritically. But to what is democracy exposed in thus exposing itself? To what other-than-democracy (what we have always called democracy) is it abandoned at its limit? In other words, is democracy only the name of the lesser evil, "the spectacle of general appropriation," or is it still that in the name of which we promise ourselves "not to let go of sense *in* common"?

Questions abandoned here, on the limit.

Community and the Limits of Theory

Christopher Fynsk

Jean-Luc Nancy begins *The Inoperative Community* with the following words:

> The gravest and most painful testimony of the modern world, which
> possibly involves all other testimonies to which this epoch must answer
> (by virtue of some unknown decree or necessity, for we bear witness
> also to the exhaustion of thinking through History), is the testimony of
> the dissolution, the dislocation, or the conflagration of community.[1]

All writing of this time, he suggests, answers in some way to this testimony, or
is gathered in it. *What is said in our time* is the absence of community.

I believe this is true. And I would like to think we were meeting here out of a
sense of urgency and distress prompted by our attention to this testimony of the
epoch. But I have to admit that I don't think this testimony is generally heard in
this community (by which I refer to a specific academic community and to the
academic community in general). And if I, for one, have been grateful to accept
the invitation to address the topic of community in this setting, it is out of a sense
of distress at a general absence of distress, and with only the faintest intimation
that as someone teaching and writing in the university, I am answering to what is
being said in our time. I do indeed think that what is being said is the absence of
community, and I agree with Jean-Luc Nancy that a *response* to this testimony —
one that truly exposes itself to it in its historical character as testimony *of our
time* — will constitute in itself the opening of another thought of community. But
I do not think that the academic discourse passing under the name of ''theory''
today (and I will use the term in this loose sense to designate generally all critical

analysis of the forms of cultural or social representation and all reflection on that analysis itself) constitutes a thinking response to this testimony.

There are, of course, many exceptions to this judgment, but I would say that the very discursive structure of "theory" as it is practiced in the university today contributes to muffle or even foreclose the testimony of the absence of community. Exceptions occur when this structure breaks down, or when it is pushed to its limits—when for some reason or other it exposes its limits. But when theory stays within its limits (and this is no less true of interdisciplinary theory), it does not hear and it does not say the absence of community. Only a kind of echo of its silencing can be heard in it. By virtue of this trace, its silence, too, belongs to the testimony of which Nancy speaks; and in this way Nancy's statement is not at all belied by the empty speech of theory. But the volume of its speech and its ubiquity in the university certainly make the testimony exceedingly difficult to hear. And I think we should be aware of the risk that this colloquium may not improve the situation—though it will be doing something if it spreads at least a sense of distress at the absence of distress.

Now, I would reiterate that if I think the language of theory silences the testimony of the absence of community, it is because the very structure of theoretical discourse prohibits it from being a language of community (I'll return to this in a moment). But I want to note as well—if only in passing, though I think the point should not be forgotten here—that if theoretical discourse in the academy is marked by an absence of distress about the absence of community, this is also for sociopolitical and institutional reasons. If time permitted (or if I had the means to do it quickly and effectively), I would want to say something about the place of theoretical discourse in the university, whose technical organization promotes or at least favors theory's silence. I would want to add a few words in turn about the isolation of the university in the United States from a larger sphere of cultural activity and about the way in which the academic disciplines concerned with culture tend to be cut off from any general public debate about the historical situation of U.S. society. I would want to say something about how the "culture of professionalism," a kind of simulacrum of community, fills the void created by this separation, and how a critical analysis undertaken apart from any ongoing engagement in public debate (or marginalized in that debate, as Said puts it in *The World, the Text, and the Critic*) will inevitably empty out—for if the criteria for a selection of topics for study and for an evaluation of research are generated solely within the sphere of academic discourse, this discourse can represent only itself.

With all of this, I would want to be saying something about the institutional conditions of what I might call the loss of the object (*die Sache, la Chose*) in the practice of theory and criticism in this country today, and I would want to relate this loss to its sociohistorical conditions: namely the place of the university in a larger cultural context where we also glimpse something like a loss of the object—the object being history. In other words, I would want to relate the absence of distress in the discourses of theory to the absence of community as it manifests itself most immediately in our culture and sociopolitical institutions. But, again, a sociohistorical analysis is required here that goes beyond my current means: one that is grounded in an analysis of our political institutions, but that is also capable of moving to a level of reflection we find in Heidegger's meditation on *Technik*, and thus at the historial level, or at the level of the question of Being. Because what we are dealing with, once again, is the loss of the object: existence in its historicity and materiality. Or perhaps not its loss, because, as my friend Rodolphe Burger once said during a visit to this country: "There's a hell of a lot of *Dasein* here." Not its loss, then, but a repression of what Nancy might call its communication, so powerful that the forces of homogenization in the dominant culture remain unsettled by it.

The qualification I have just made about the loss of the object in the culture in the United States should also be made about theoretical and critical discourse in the university. While I can't quite give up my adherence to the statement from which I started, I sense also that it indulges in what Jean-François Lyotard might term piety. It would be misleading to suggest that the voice of community (which today says the absence of community and is thus calling for another thought of community) is not speaking in all sorts of ways and at all sorts of sites in the field of theory. The problem is rather that in general it is not heard as such and meditated upon as a testimony of community and as saying something about our historical situation. It would also be misleading, indeed it would be misguided, to suggest that the only discourse contributing to the struggle to liberate the communication of existence in its historicity and materiality is one that seeks to effect that communication. We cannot do without theory: that is to say, we cannot do without a *representation* of our sociohistorical situation and we cannot do without the forceful representation of political positions. But if we limit our understanding of critical discourse to its representational or interpretive function, then we cannot conceive of its political import outside the bounds of what Richard Rorty has called "edification."

To illustrate what I am saying about the limits of theoretical or critical discourse when it limits itself to the task of interpretation (even when "interpretation" is understood as being always the interpretation of other interpretations), I would like to pause over Rorty's definition of this term, "edification." The notion is perhaps somewhat simplistic (for "pragmatic" reasons, we might say), but nevertheless extremely revealing about pragmatic assumptions concerning language—assumptions that inform, I believe, a large portion of theoretical and critical activity in this country, and thus contribute to inhibiting reflection on community as Nancy has tried to define the term. (If time permitted, it would also be appropriate to show how these assumptions inform Rorty's "liberalism"—I leave the term to its ambiguity—and his apology for North

American socioeconomic institutions; but I would also have to add that the same assumptions inform more severe and more progressive cultural criticism.)

Rorty uses the term ''edification'' in his volume *Philosophy and the Mirror of Nature* (357–72)[2] in order to designate the function of philosophy in a ''postphilosophical context'' (that is, after the collapse of foundational philosophy)—a context in which philosophy would no longer hold a privileged point of view in the search for a community's self-representation, but would join literature and the other discourses of culture in what Rorty calls a ''conversation.'' ''Edification'' has a dual meaning in this postphilosophical perspective. It designates: (1) the elaboration of the best possible representation of a community's historical situation and goals, and (2) the critical practice of demonstrating that this representation (like all representations) is only a possible representation. Accordingly, Rorty recognizes two modes of edifying philosophy: the ''hermeneutic'' and the ''therapeutic.''[3] By the former, Rorty refers to a practice of interpretation conceived roughly on the model of Gadamerian dialogue and consisting of a movement between the ''incommensurable'' discourses of a culture or cultures. The discourses of a culture are ''incommensurable'' not in principle, according to Rorty, but rather, if one may say so, by lack of principle—that is to say, by reason of the lack of criteria with which one might evaluate the truth-claims of one discourse in relation to another. We have, for example, no transcendental vantage point that would allow us to arbitrate between the descriptions of man provided by anthropology, by cybernetics, by philosophy, or by literature. Nor do we have any justification, in Rorty's view, for arguing that such discourses are irreducible to one another or in principle incomparable; by ''incommensurable'' Rorty means simply that no comparison is possible in the sense that each discourse could be evaluated in relation to a common measure furnished by a formal analysis of language or a theory of representation. A hermeneutic passage between discourses is possible, therefore, even a synthesis—but this synthesis does not provide the truth of the discourses in question. Its truth-value will be determined solely by consensus in the light of its internal cohesion and its extension: the quantity of data it allows us to account for. Hermeneutics is therefore a way of ''seeing how things hang together'' without seeking their rational grounding—a weaving of discourses at the service of the community's tasks of self-definition (or self-formation: *Bildung*) and self-affirmation.

Rorty's definition of the second mode of edification, what I am calling ''therapeutic philosophy,'' is in fact contained in that of the first. ''Therapeutic philosophy'' represents the critical moment in edification that renders possible the work of hermeneutics as a conversation between incommensurable discourses. It conducts the critique of representation that liberates hermeneutics from the constraint of reference and recalls to this same hermeneutics that its representations are historically conditioned interpretations that are always subject to revision. In this critical function, therapeutic philosophy is always ''secondary'' or ''parasitic" in relation to the production of representations in the hermeneutic process. It serves merely to keep the conversation open by "denaturalizing" any language or discourse that threatens to impose itself as the language of nature itself — *the* language that gives access to things in their truth. It serves to protect against any epistemological or foundational temptation, and consequently the style proper to it is satire, parody, and aphorism. For Rorty, the heroes of this style are Nietzsche, Wittgenstein, Heidegger, and Derrida.

Rorty thus defines (and seeks to contain) the critique of the metaphysics of representation developed in modern Continental philosophy as the "negative" moment within the dialectics of edification (a hermeneutic activity opened and kept in motion by a therapeutic auto-critique — the latter always in the service of the former). But to do so he must leave aside everything in this critique that would bring into question his essentially instrumentalist view of language and the pragmatist assumption that the horizon of human linguistic activity is that of the communicable meaning established in consensus by free subjects. Those familiar with the "therapeutic" texts in question will recognize that what Rorty leaves aside is thus nothing other than the key elements of the philosophy of language elaborated in them: in general, all thought of the historical (and ontological — in Heidegger's vocabulary, "historial") conditions of the production of meaning and of the subject's signifying activity. Rorty accepts the notion that language is constitutive of experience, but he understands this to mean that the subject constitutes the meaning of its experience — not, as the "therapeutic" authors suggest, that language is in some sense *constitutive of the subject*. In a word, Rorty would save from the critique of representation the subject of representation itself.

We see Rorty's effort to limit the thrust of the critique of representation in a passage in which he attempts to group Wittgenstein and Heidegger together as examples of therapeutic edifying philosophers. Rorty has named Nietzsche and Heidegger and is discussing how such authors are attacked by traditional philosophers for not practicing "philosophy":

> The problem for an edifying philosopher is that *qua* philosopher he is in the business of offering arguments, whereas he would like simply to offer another set of terms, *without* saying that these terms are the new-found accurate representations of essences. . . . He is, so to speak, violating not just the rules of normal philosophy (the philosophy of the schools of his day) but a sort of meta-rule: the rule that one may suggest changing the rules only because one has noticed that the old ones do not fit the subject matter, that they are not adequate to reality, that they impede the solution of the eternal problems. . . . They refuse to present themselves as having found out any objective philosophy. They present themselves as doing something different from, and more important than, offering accurate representations of how things are. It is more important because, they say, the notion of "accurate

representation'' itself is not the proper way to think about what philosophy does. . . . Whereas less pretentious revolutionaries can afford to have views on lots of things which their predecessors had views on, edifying philosophers have to decry the very notion of having a view, while avoiding having a view about having views. This is an awkward, but not impossible position. Wittgenstein and Heidegger manage it fairly well. One reason they manage it as well as they do is that they do not think that when we say something we must necessarily be expressing a view about a subject. We might just be *saying something* — participating in a conversation rather than contributing to an inquiry. Perhaps saying things is not always saying how things are. Perhaps saying *that* is itself not a case of saying how things are. Both men suggest we see people as saying things, better or worse things, without seeing them as externalizing inner representations of reality. . . . We have to drop the notion of correspondence for sentences as well as for thoughts, and see sentences as connected with other sentences rather than with the world. (*Philosophy*, 370–72)

Rorty's point here is fairly clear. The therapeutic edifying philosopher is one who carries out the critique of representation and applies it to his own critique — seeking to avoid setting in place a representation of the true nature of representation. Rorty acknowledges that these philosophers think they are doing something other and more important than representation, but since Rorty wants to avoid suggesting that there is any positive dimension to their activity, he limits his examples of this ''something other'' to the production of a nonthetic declaration — a simple *that* (as in the case of Heidegger), or a speaking that would have only to make us understand that it is just speaking and that words draw their meaning from other words and not from their relations to things. (I'll return in a moment to this neutralizing gesture.) In the paragraph that follows the passage I have just cited, Rorty concludes by asking what attitude is appropriate before a philosopher that refuses to posit anything: ''How do we know when to adopt a tactful attitude and when to insist on someone's moral obligation to hold a view?'' And he responds that we never know: ''This is like asking how we know when someone's refusal to adopt our norms (or, for example, social organization, sexual practice, or conversational manners) is morally outrageous and when it is something we must respect (at least provisionally). We do not know such things by reference to general principles'' (372). So in the case of therapeutic edifying philosophers, as in our political context, our decision will depend on the situation and on our social needs. In a moment of social crisis, it may be that we cannot tolerate the behavior of an edifying philosopher, just as we cannot tolerate the behavior of a social deviant, but the preferable situation in Rorty's eyes is to seek conversation rather than exclusion (and Rorty presupposes that conversation never, in principle, implies violence).

Now, it is interesting to see how Rorty's liberal attitude is strained when he enters into an overtly political discussion and when it comes to dealing with authors like Gilles Deleuze and Jean-François Lyotard. Once again, he refuses to their use of language any positive dimension, but he finds no useful therapeutic dimension in their writing. He argues that research that takes on the accents of the tragic or the sublime and seeks to expose the precariousness of a regime or order of meaning by putting into play the possibility of transgression or transcendence can only be seen as responding to the personal and idiosyncratic needs of the individuals who undertake it.[4] For Rorty, the social bond — which he thinks of essentially in terms of identification (Foucault gets bad marks for a failure to identify) and such notions as "shared confidence" and "shared hope" — has its source in and develops with the conversation that unfolds in the horizon of a consensus of communication. This conversation is guided, he says, by the desire to achieve a social harmony in which a society "affirms itself globally," though without seeking to found itself. One might ask, I think, whether the desire for "global affirmation" is finally separable from the desire for auto-foundation. (The connection here is the concept of will — the fundamental trait of the modern subject of representation: Heidegger's reading of Nietzsche is invaluable here, and particularly as it reflects upon his own statements in his "Rectoral Address" of 1933.[5] I would note too that if we bring together Rorty's statements on hermeneutics as *Bildung*, and consider Rorty's faith in our freedom to change our representations, we see that we have to do in his thinking with all the basic traits of the subject of metaphysics: freedom, imagination, will. Once again, an attentive reading will show that Rorty employs the critique of representation to shore up the subject of representation.) In other words, one might ask whether his notion of consensus does not finally participate in the phantasms of identification and unification at work in the modern forms of tyranny.

But I am less interested here in the dangers of Rorty's notion of consensus than I am in the nature of what he chooses to marginalize or neutralize with his aggressive dismissals of discourses with a political agenda that seek to interrupt or exceed the horizon of signification. And I would like to suggest that what Rorty is combatting in the name of consensus (which he calls at one point, "the vital force" of a culture ["Habermas, Lyotard et la postmodernité," 196]) is the ethical dimension of a writing practice that works at the limits of representation — and ultimately another thought of the grounds of community.

I am using the word "ethical" here in the light of Wittgenstein's "Lecture on Ethics," in which Wittgenstein considers the possibility of what I might call an "ethical language" or a language that expresses what he calls his ethical experience par excellence.[6] This experience is one that recurs, he says, every time he tries to grasp what is meant by ethical value. "The best way to describe it," he writes, "is to say that when I have it, I wonder at the existence of the world" (8). The experience, in other words, is the same experience Heidegger tries to express in the phrase "that there are beings, and not nothing"—and there is textual evidence suggesting that when Wittgenstein meditates on the possibility of an ethical language, he is in fact meditating on Heidegger's claims for this very phrase.[7] Heidegger had suggested that when the phrase "that there are beings, and not nothing" comes to us in the uncanny experience of the Nothing, it gives the possibility of saying "is"—and thus a relation to ourselves, to others, and to everything that is. The phrase itself, he said, marks the very possibility of signification, and gives the "is" (*"Das es seiendes* ist") in an originary fashion—it says the possibility of significant language, and thus, in a sense, gives language itself. Heidegger will later call such an event the speaking of language. Now, it is to such an event that Wittgenstein himself points when he offers the hypothesis that the only possible expression of the miraculous fact of the existence of the world is the presentation of language itself: "I am tempted to say that the right expression *in* language for the miracle of the existence of the world, though it is not any proposition in language, is the existence of language itself ("Lecture on Ethics" 11). The "correct" expression for the experience of the fact *that there is something* would be the expression provided by the existence of language itself—or, in other words, the presentation of the fact *that there is language*. When language gives itself as such, there is a saying of Being—the fact that there is something rather than nothing.

Wittgenstein does not go as far as Heidegger—he does not suggest, as does Heidegger, that such a saying would mark and remark the opening of our relation to what is, and play in some sense a constitutive role in this experience. In other words, he does not suggest that ethical language (if such a thing could be achieved—and Wittgenstein is not sure it could be, though he expresses admiration for all attempts) would be the condition of ethical experience. But he does say something that anticipates Heidegger's later turn to the work of art and the language of poetry as the site where the event he is describing presents itself or remarks itself (in other words, as the site—or a site—where language remarks the fact of its existence). He says, near the beginning of his lecture, that much of what he will have to say about ethics might normally fall into the realm of aesthetics. He says this in part because he designates his ethical experience as sublime, but also because he is meditating on something like a sublime use of language: he is meditating on the possibility of presenting what properly speaking cannot be presented because it is the condition of all presentation or representation.

Let me go back now to Rorty. When Rorty cited Heidegger's "that" as an instance of a "therapeutic" edifying language, he was pointing to what both Wittgenstein and Heidegger were attempting to define as a language at the limit of signification. But he left aside entirely the question of what happens when a discourse works at that limit; he left it aside because Rorty finally cannot entertain seriously language that is not representational—its value for him is at best "therapeutic." So he left aside, or simply could not see, Heidegger's (and Wittgenstein's) suggestion that when a discourse produces in some manner the "that," it is saying something of language itself—that the essence of language is speaking by remarking the very possibility of signification or representation.

If time allowed, I would try to explore some examples of the kind of strangeness that marks a discourse when it produces the equivalent of Heidegger's "that." I would point to Blanchot's notion of language becoming an image of itself, and try to describe the properly sublime character of some of his fiction. I would point to Derrida's notion of the "*retrait*" of metaphor that remarks the fundamental metaphoricity of Being itself. I would dwell upon what Nancy calls "voice," and I would be tempted to consider in the light of this notion the strange authority that characterized some of Paul de Man's work, and particularly his extraordinary verbal performances. Each of these examples points to ways in which language might address us or claim us when it "speaks"—and will perhaps give some sense of what I will finally have wanted to suggest by saying that only a criticism that is held by language can be said to be answering to the writing of community as Nancy defines it.

A critical or theoretical language that is *held* by language, I want to suggest, is one that answers to the speaking of language—that answers to what it is about a text or discourse that remarks the fact of language and thereby says the possibility of its own representing or signifying. This saying, of course, is not itself a signifying. Once again, what is said is the possibility of signification. Nancy defined such a saying in *Le Partage des voix* as a *hermeneia*: an annunciation of meaning that is originary because its speaking is the opening of meaning—a singular articulation of the communitary logos (which *is* only in its articulations). So criticism that is held by the language of a text, for example, is thus one that answers to the text's own *hermeneia*—it allows itself to be claimed by what constitutes the singularity of the text. And I would like to suggest that any effective criticism—that is to say, a criticism that becomes political in the sense defined by Nancy in *La Communauté désoeuvrée*—is one that answers by effecting in its turn a *hermeneia*.

If we follow Nancy's argument concerning the singularity of any act that says the possibility of signification (and Nancy is in strict conformity with Heidegger on this point), then we would have to acknowledge, in fact, that any criticism or interpretation that exposes in a text the *hermeneia* of that text, its saying of the opening of meaning it effects, is itself a *hermeneia*. It could not be the simple reception and re-presentation of the address of the text it reads, but must produce in its turn, and in response, a singular speaking of language. It must divide the *logos* in its turn. There could be no opening to the opening of meaning that did not itself articulate meaning in an originary fashion.[8] Heidegger would put it this way: The response to language that brings language to speak must be thought as anticipatory—both receptive, and, I would say, *provocative*. The response to language has of necessity a performative dimension—it provokes the address. So any criticism that answers in this sense to the writing of community will be in its turn the writing of community.

I approached the task of writing this paper by asking myself the following question: If theoretical discourse silences the testimony of the absence of community, what language would respond to this testimony and answer thereby to the political reality of our time? What would a politically effective language *be* in the disciplines that concern most immediately the majority of those of us here: the disciplines concerned with the forms of cultural representation, and more particularly literature, conceived in a large sense? I hope that the response I want to offer will be intelligible now. It is essentially the same one Benjamin gave to Martin Buber when Buber asked him to contribute to his journal *Der Jude* (and thus engage in "political writing" in the usual sense of the term).[9] Politically effective language, Benjamin responded, is one that acts in language and by language: not as an instrument or means for the communication of some signified content, but rather as a kind of intervention in language by which the essence of language itself is brought into play. Now, Benjamin's terms for such a language would seem to lead away from any properly political reflection: he speaks in his letter of its "mystery" or "magic," and invokes his concept of "pure language." But what he is referring to, I believe, is the same thing Heidegger refers to when he speaks of the essence of language and the effort to bring it to speech. Once again, when language itself is brought to speak, as Heidegger understands this event, it gives itself as the site where our relation to what is is defined: our relation to ourselves, to other human beings, and to everything that is. It gives itself, in other words, as the site where the always communitary definition of what it means to be is articulated. This is the articulation of what I called at the outset the object or the thing: existence in its historicity and materiality—and it is constantly being articulated in multiple and always singular signifying acts. To engage in that process, if only in the process of remarking it, is a political act—it is to attend to the voice of the community and to make it heard. But as we have seen, there is no simple remarking or observation of this process. To engage with the process is to intervene in it. When theory or criticism answer to language, they become a practice: the writing of community.

Notes

1. Jean-Luc Nancy, *The Inoperative Community*, ed. Peter Connor, trans. Peter Connor, Lisa Garbus, Michael Holland, and Simona Sawhney (Minneapolis: University of Minnesota Press, 1991), 1.

2. See Chapter 8, 357–72. In these remarks on Rorty's notion of "edification," I am drawing from work presented in my essay "Freiheit der Interpretation im liberalen Amerika," trans. Thomas Kleinbub, in *Tumult* (Munich: Klaus Boer, 1987), 125–32.

3. I use these designations for heuristic purposes, and should note that the distinction between "hermeneutic" and "therapeutic" is effectively lost when Rorty undertakes to distinguish between

"edifying" philosophers and "systematic" philosophers in the pages from *Philosophy and the Mirror of Nature* (Princeton: Princeton University Press, 1982) to which I have referred. But the distinction is nevertheless necessary to Rorty's effort to marginalize or neutralize the more radical dimension of the critique of representation, and can be seen at work throughout his readings of the "edifying" philosophers. In the light of Rorty's reference to a literary or poetic dimension in "edification" (360), "interpretive" may be preferable to "hermeneutic." But I retain the latter term because "edification" is proposed in *Philosophy and the Mirror of Nature* as a translation for *Bildung* as Gadamer has defined the term. The term "therapeutic" is used in the introduction to *Philosophy and the Mirror of Nature* (5–7). For Rorty's notion of "edification" in a "post-philosophical" culture, see also the introduction to *Consequences of Pragmatism* (Minneapolis: University of Minnesota Press, 1982), xiii–xlvii.

4. I am moving quickly in this passage through material contained in "Method, Social Science, Social Hope" (*Consequences of Pragmatism*, 191–210), "Solidarité ou objectivité," (*Critique*, 39, no. 439, 923–40); "Habermas, Lyotard et la postmodernité," (*Critique*, 40, no. 442, 181–97); and "Le Cosmopolitisme sans émancipation: en réponse à Jean-François Lyotard" (*Critique*, 41, no. 456, 569–80). All of these essays, but particularly the last, offer perspectives on Rorty's thought of community and points to the political dimension of his project.

5. Martin Heidegger, *Die Selbstbehauptung der deutschen Universität* (Breslau: Korn, 1933). In his essay "Solidarité ou objectivité" (939), Rorty cites approvingly Hans Blumenberg's effort to distinguish *Selbstbehauptung* ("self-assertion"; translated in French as "auto-affirmation") from *Selbstbegründung*. But I would argue that Rorty's reliance on a notion of will renders this distinction problematic.

6. I have discussed Wittgenstein's "Lecture" (published in *Philosophical Review*, 74, 3-27) in an unpublished essay, "*Qu'il y a le langage* . . . :Heidegger, Derrida."

7. I refer to Friedrich Waismann's transcription of remarks made by Wittgenstein on December 30, 1929, translated in their entirety (that is, with the references to Heidegger restored that were omitted in the original English translation) by Michael Murray in *Heidegger and Modern Philosophy* (New Haven: Yale University Press, 1982), 80–83. The phrase from Heidegger appears in "What Is Metaphysics?", a text that circulated widely in 1929.

8. Thus while the criticism I am describing will be held by the language of a text, it will not simply submit to it. I use the metaphor of a "hold" in order to counter the common (supposedly Nietzschean) notion of the "freedom" of interpretation. But it will be apparent that the initiative taken by the writing I am describing also calls for a new notion of freedom.

9. Philippe Lacoue-Labarthe cites much of this letter in the introduction to Walter Benjamin, *Le Concept de critique esthétique dans le romantisme allemand* (Paris: Flammarion, 1986), 11–13.

Communism, the Proper Name

Georges Van Den Abbeele

I would like to speak about names, about the politics of names, and about the politics of a particular name.

Section 92 of Jean-François Lyotard's *Differend* brings to a provisional close a long development, which in light of its debt to Saul Kripke could be entitled "Naming and Contingency." As part of a general strategy to counter those revisionist historians like Robert Faurisson who would deny the existence of the Holocaust, Lyotard seeks to reorient the criteria for historico-political reality away from the easily refutable and vulnerable testimony of eyewitnesses and toward the rigorous triangulation of phrases that identify the existence of a referent to the extent that it is not only displayed but also signified and named (no. 65). The assertion of reality cannot be, as it no doubt was for Dr. Johnson in his "refutation" of Bishop Berkeley (Boswell 1: 471), simply a function of a deixis that points to an *object of perception* in a phenomenological *field*. For that assertion to occur with validity, an ostensive phrase must be linked onto a nominative one, i.e., one whose referent is an *object of history* situated in a *world* (no. 81). While deixis is only valid for the phrase in which it occurs (one's *here* is another's *there*; my *you* is your *I*, etc.), names, which are "a pure mark of the designative function," remain the same across phrases, from whose actualizations they accordingly remain "independent" (no. 57). They are, to use Kripke's phrase, "rigid designators," and as such, function as what Lyotard calls "quasi-deictics":

Networks of quasi-deictics formed by names of "objects" and by names of relations designate "givens" and the relations between those givens, that is to say, a world. I call it a world because those names, being "rigid," each refer to something even when that something is not there; and because that something is considered to be the same for all phrases which refer to it by its name; and also because each of those names is independent of the phrase universes that refer to it, and in particular of the addressors and addressees presented in those universes. This is not to say that something which has the same name in several phrases has the same meaning. Different descriptions can be made of it, and the question of its cognition is opened and not closed by its name. (no. 60)

That a name can receive any number of meanings introduces a certain contingency into the relations between field and world. If reality occurs as a "swarm of senses light[ing] upon a field pinpointed by a world" (no. 82), then "reality is not a matter of the absolute eyewitness, but a matter of the future" (no. 88). In contradistinction to essentialist notions, which understand "the referent of the name as if it were the referent of a definition" (no. 88)—that is, as a shorthand for a bundle of preinscribed qualities—Lyotard sees the number of possible senses ascribable to a named referent as bounded only by the contingency of the future (no. 89). The predicate, *passes the Rubicon*, is not, as Leibniz thinks (310–11), necessarily preinscribed in the notion of Caesar, since the "referent of the name *Caesar* is not a completely describable essence, even with Caesar dead" (no. 88, cf. no. 74). It cannot be determined in advance how many or which meanings can be validated for a particular name. The senses of a named referent refer us not to the *field* of perception but to the *world* of history, and as such, to an agonistic locus of debate, litigation, antagonism, and differend. That the (historically contingent) link between name and meaning ushers in the political is what section 92 brings to the fore:

Reality entails the differend. *That's Stalin, here he is.* We acknowledge it. But as for what *Stalin* means? Phrases come to be attached to this name, which not only describe different senses for it (this can still be debated in dialogue), and not only place the name on different instances, but which also obey heterogeneous regimens and/or genres. This heterogeneity, for lack of a common idiom, makes consensus impossible. The assignment of a definition to Stalin necessarily does wrong to the nondefinitional phrases relating to Stalin, which this definition, for a while at least, disregards or betrays. In and around names, vengeance is on the prowl. Forever?

What does it mean, though, for vengeance to be "on the prowl" in and around names? The answer is elaborated in Lyotard's long essay "Judiciousness in Dispute, or Kant after Marx." There, we read:

> [Vengeance] can invoke no right, for right is always "right" according
> to a tribunal that is unique and that demands proofs, names, and
> measurements. What cries out for vengeance are the forbidden phrases
> of defense, phrases that have suffered a wrong because they can only
> make an appeal to feelings. . . . The authority of the idiom in which
> cases are established and regulated is contested. A different idiom and a
> different tribunal are demanded, which the other party contests and
> rejects. Language is at war with itself, and the critical watchman posts
> guard over this war. The name "Palestine" belongs to several worlds of
> names. Within each of these worlds, several regimes of phrases quarrel
> over the name "Palestine." Here we have an analogon of language: not
> simply the complexity of a large city but the complexity of a large city
> at war. In 1956, at Budapest, the names of the streets were changed to
> mislead the Soviet tanks; the government doesn't change peoples, the
> people change names: this is the clandestine. And this is why
> philosophy must remain in arms. (64–65)

It would not be difficult, at this point, to multiply examples, and hence to disclose a very rich terrain of historico-political analysis. One would have to consider, among others, the invention, attribution, substitution, effacement, and appropriation of names.

I'm reminded, for instance, of a recent British film entitled precisely *Naming the Names*, in which the Irish heroine responds to her interrogator's request for the names of IRA members by enumerating the streets of Belfast. And as the very sense of names remains indefinite, the struggles in question may not, by any means, be resolved. Consider the case of the autochthonous inhabitants of the Western Hemisphere, variously termed Indians or Native Americans, terms that reveal either Columbus's reductive misprision or the projective appropriation of the name of his colleague Amerigo (cf. O'Gorman, Todorov 1–50). To underscore the point, consider if the first European explorer of the North American coastline, Giovanni da Verrazanno, had been better received by his benefactor, Francis I of France. In the latter's honor, Verrazanno called what is now the Eastern seaboard of the United States, Francesca. We would be speaking today of the United States of Francesca, and its indigenous peoples would be called Native Francescans. Or, consider the name of Miami University of Ohio, always at pains to distinguish itself from the Floridian city of the same name. In their currency today, however, both names occlude even as they designate the historical passage of those from whom this name was taken, as do so many other indigenous place-names in the Western Hemisphere, unwitting signs of an absence no longer even felt as absent. As for the once mighty Miami Indian nation that ruled a vast territory between the Alleghenies and the Mississippi, its members were progressively subjugated, annihilated, assimilated, or deported to those places that received the name of that people as the tearful trail of their passage: the county of

Miami, Kansas, and still farther off, the town of Miami, Oklahoma (Anson, Carter).

Before what court could the autochthonous dweller of America bring the claim of a wrong done to him or her on account of being *called* "American"? An international jury would have no jurisdiction since the case would be seen to involve a dispute between two Americans, and so, the case would be sent back to an American court, who would by definition see no grounds for the complaint since the so-called American Indian would be viewed as but a duly enfranchised American. In *The Differend*, Lyotard elaborates this dilemma in the case of the Martinican (no. 36), but the same could also be said of the Québécois or so-called French Canadian, the Palestinian, the Basque, the Namibian, the Azanian, the Katangan, and countless others with or without names.

But if we are thus led to understand the political through a generalized agonistics of the name, then the stakes involved in what meanings can or cannot be attributed to a proper name, in how that name can or cannot occur in certain phrases, become very high. And the philosophical stakes in knowing what constitutes a proper name become just as high. Are there not certain common nouns that are also at issue in differends? In other words, how is the proper name as contested in a differend to be distinguished from debate over the meaning and usage of any word or concept? This was the question I posed to Jean-François Lyotard some time ago, and to which he answered as follows:

> Proper names have that property of attracting to themselves phrases belonging to different regimens and to heterogeneous genres of discourse: *Caesar, for pity's sake! Down with Caesar! Caesar was at that time consul. Was Caesar a great writer? Your Caesar annoys me.* It is for this reason that the differend flourishes in and around proper names. A "debate" over the signification of a common noun is a genre strictly regulated in its end (the establishment of a definition) and in its procedures (dialogue). The difference between one and the other is the one noted by Aristotle at the beginning of the *Rhetoric*, shall we say: the difference between School and political life, which tears apart the man of knowledge or of litigation, at the tribune, at the tribunal or out in the street, the agonistical places. ("Interview," 20)

Clearly, the allocation of sense to a common noun *can* take place as a regulated debate within disciplinary boundaries. The agonistics of academic "dialogue" already presupposes the existence of a set of common idioms, practices, interests, and institutional parameters, which frame disagreement, for instance, over what anthropology is or what the liberal arts are. Whether phenomenological or ontological, such disagreements enter the political and the historical only with the advent of names. Hence, academic debates over deconstruction as a practice of literary criticism link up with heterogeneous genres of discourse, say journalism, when questions (of a different order) are raised as to what sense should be granted the named referent, Paul de Man.[1] This is not because the meaning of this name cannot be determined by and within the genre of academic discussion (hence, the anxiety and/or outrage felt by many literary professionals that the discussion is not restricted to this genre), but because the name *can* always attract other senses by its ability to stay the same while being situated differently according to *different* phrase regimens and genres of discourse. A debate over the composition of a molecule, however, can only occur within a discourse that allows such an object to emerge as an object of perception: chemistry, for instance. As such, "there are no true discussions" (no. 152).

It seems important at this time to refine the notion of the name further by deflecting any anthropologizing that would view the distinction between proper name and common noun as if it were one between persons and things. For Lyotard, the name is a "pure mark of the designative function" (no. 57)—hence whatever in language refers rather than signifies—in Peircian terms, the indexical rather than the symbolic (2: 156–73), or *Bedeutung* rather than *Sinn*, to use the Fregian terms that have informed Lyotard's thinking on language since at least *Discours, figure*. To quote again from *The Differend*: "Names transform *now* into a date, *here* into a place, *I, you, he* into Jean, Pierre, Louis. . . . Names grouped into calendars, cartographical systems, genealogies and civil statutes are indicators of possible reality. They present their referents, dates, places and human beings as givens" (no. 58). Names are quasi-deictics that designate rigidly across phrase regimens and genres of discourse, and the network of names pinpoints the world of *historical* objects. But are there not historical objects that arise from this world and that are not names, or at least not names in the usual sense of the word?

I must admit that when I put to Jean-François Lyotard the question of the limits of the proper name, I had something particular in mind, something whose definition as object was not readily containable within the framework of a disciplinary debate, and hence was—indeed still is—very much a matter for differends; something, though, which carried along a considerable amount of *Sinn* in its *Bedeutung* and thus was not merely designative. I had in mind the name of a historical movement or event that was also a theory, if not a vision. This historical and political movement bore a name that was also a common noun, indeed the noun of commonality itself or of what is held in common, namely communism.

That communism is not just a "concept" or even "the *sense* of a word" is corroborated by Jean-Luc Nancy near the beginning of *La Communauté désoeuvrée* (12) when he refers to the word communism as an "emblem," one that has gone out of circulation. At one time, however, it would have emblematized "the desire for a locus of community found or refound over and beyond social divisions and over and beyond subjection to techno-political domination" (11). Such a desire, according to Nancy, would invariably maintain a view of human community as a "community of beings in essence producing their own essence as their work and, what is more, producing this essence precisely *as community*" (14). To the extent, then, that the community is based on the self-production of itself as community, communism would remain entrenched in exactly the same immanentism as that which plagues humanism with its essentialist supposition of man giving birth to himself. To the extent that this immanent view of the social reduces individual differences (or singularities) to the mere expression of an essence subtending the community, the resulting allegory of tautology, or "tautegory" (130), would issue in a totalitarian state. The historical apparition of such states that have manifestly betrayed the revolution would mean that the assertion Nancy imputes to Sartre that "communism is the insuperable horizon of our time" will have lost all currency.[2] In what we could then call the "current" situation or climate of resignation, everything would be, to quote Nancy, "as if the disappearance, impossibility, or condemnation of communism . . . had formed the new insuperable horizon" (28). Nancy justifiably rejects such a view: "That's why, while positing that communism is no longer our insuperable horizon, it is also necessary to posit, with just as much force, that a communist exigency communicates with the gesture according to which we ought to go beyond all horizons" (28).

It would seem to be in accordance with such a "communist exigency," then, that Nancy seeks to formulate an alternative not only to the problem of community as an essence immanent to itself but also to that other immanence, which would view community as but the (harmonious or disharmonious or contractual) aggregate of preexisting and self-generating "individuals." Radically rejecting the priority of either individual or community to the other, Nancy proposes instead to develop a communitarian logic derived from the *relation* of "being-in-common" (see also his text by that title in this volume).

This relation, as inescapable as it is indeterminate, is not just a relation of commonality (i.e., what we all have in common) but more significantly, what we share in common at the limit of commonality or community, namely the incommunicable commonality of our finitudes: birth, death, and no doubt a good deal in between. It is from this "community at loose ends," produced in its unproduction or instituted in its destitution (*dés-oeuvrée*) that the social and political must be thought. What Nancy thus calls, in a combination of eloquence and provocation, "literary communism" (a term he has since renounced) is precisely not some mythic community or communion that would have been lost in some Golden Age. Nor is it something that is ours yet to invent through some kind of immanent expression. Rather, it is what inaugurates the communal relation, what precedes us not as our foundation or destiny but precisely as our being (in common) at loose ends (*La Communauté désoeuvrée*, 169–98). Nancy's communism is thus neither a past nor a future classless society but precisely the *neces-*

sary liminality of the social, which is also a point of resistance that inscribes the ineradicable contingency of difference.

Such a literary (or perhaps it should be called liminal) communism would, then, be the name of a limit as well as a limit of the name. Undecidably concept and name, communism is also historically the name of a struggle to overcome a set of property relations, specifically the relations of production under capitalism. Hence, its call for the abolition of private property in order to arrest the extraction of surplus value by those who own the means of production from those who have nothing to sell but their labor power. The name of the struggle is also the name of the relation that the struggle desires to institute: communism.

In order to do this, however, this name of a relation must also become a relation of names. In *Hegemony and Socialist Strategy*, Ernesto Laclau and Chantal Mouffe (who, by the way, alternate their spelling of communism, now with a capital, now with a small *c*) analyze what at first seems like a merely amusing epiphenomenon of official communist rhetoric, namely the practice of enumeration. But, as they warn us, "to enumerate is never an innocent operation; it involves major displacements of meaning" (62–63). The practice of communist enumeration (or rather, the communist practice of enumeration) arose during the 1930s and 1940s, that is, during the great era of Popular Fronts and struggles for decolonization, when, as they explain, the "common ground of democracy was not open to exclusive absorption by any one social sector" or class (62) — that is, when the fight against the various fascisms and imperialisms required a mobilization beyond what could be mustered by the specific interests of any single group, none of which could claim itself to be the sole representative of democratic aspirations. As Laclau and Mouffe further specify: "Communist enumeration occurs within a dichotomic space that establishes the antagonism between dominant and popular sectors; and the identity of both is constructed on the basis of enumerating their constitutive class sectors. On the side of the popular sectors, for example, would be included: the working class, the peasantry, the petty bourgeoisie, the progressive factions of the national bourgeoisie, etc." (63). The enumeration of elements allied in the popular struggle is not, however, "the discursive expression of a real movement constituted outside discourse; on the contrary, this enumerative discourse is a real force which contributes to the moulding and constitution of social relations" (110). Communist enumeration is not, if one likes, constative but virulently performative in character: it marshals or articulates the social forces engaged in a common struggle in a way that potentially undermines or blocks the dominance of any one group in leading the struggle. As such, the enumerative practice of communism is of crucial import to Laclau and Mouffe in their reconceptualization of the Gramscian notion of hegemony on a basis that is no longer class specific.

It also provides them with one of their most important theoretical concepts, the "expansive logic of equivalences," a notion whose first mention and definition occur right on the heels of the discussion of enumeration, and which appears then as a logical clarification of that practice:

> This enumeration, however, does not merely affirm the separate and literal *presence* of certain classes or class fractions at the popular pole; it also asserts their *equivalence* in the common confrontation with the dominant pole. A relation of equivalence is not a relation of identity among objects. Equivalence is never tautological, as the substitutability it establishes among certain objects is only valid for determinate positions within a given structural context. In this sense, equivalence displaces the identity which makes it possible, from the objects themselves to the contexts of their appearance or presence. This, however, means that in the relation of equivalence the identity of the object is split: on the one hand, it maintains its own "literal" sense; on the other, it symbolizes the contextual position for which it is a substitutable element. This is exactly what occurs in the communist enumeration: from a strictly classist point of view, there is no identity whatsoever among the sectors of the popular pole, given that each one has differentiated and even antagonistic interests; yet, the relation of equivalence established among them, in the context of their opposition to the dominant pole, constructs a "popular" discursive position that is irreducible to class positions. (63)

The constitution of the hegemonic bloc through the logic of equivalences soon enters, however, into the same dilemma as that raised by Nancy in his critique of community, namely the dilemma between the immanence of each part to itself within a loose or contractual aggregate, on the one hand, and the immanence of the whole reducing each part to but a manifestation of itself, on the other hand. Residual definitions and categories appear in ensuing distinctions between equivalence and "total" equivalence (or the collapse of all difference between equivalential terms into an identity built on their effacement; cf. 127–34) and later in the book's closing dialectic between the logic of equivalence and its counterpoised logic of autonomy (181ff.). The earliest formulation of the problem occurs as the split, on pages 64–65, between democratic and authoritarian forms of communism, between a liberating and differentiating practice of "articulation" that "accepts the structural diversity of the relations in which social agents are immersed" (65) and a repressive and reductive practice of "representation" that "denies all opacity and density to political relations" (65) by grasping each enumerative instance as but the representation of another "until a final class core is reached which supposedly gives meaning to the whole series" (65). In those states, then, that have come to be called "communist," the logic of equivalences has tended to be subtended by the state bureaucracy of a "party" representing itself as the vanguard of a particular class (the proletariat) that, in turn, is understood to be the representative of all other social sectors. However, this collapse from equivalence into *total* equivalence entails the abandonment of equivalential logic for the representational one that both supersedes and subtends the set of differing elements, which are ipso facto reduced to being mere *moments* within the ultimate suturing of a closed society, transparent unto itself.

To translate the problem into the idiom that is Lyotard's, the phrasing of the social as enumeration places the entities it names simultaneously in the positions of addressor, addressee, and referent. The tautegorical risk of this construction is inscribed in the possibility of the sense component being seen as identical with a meta-addressor who would speak for the whole of those named and who would then name itself as the *sense* of their identity. This is recognizably the moment of Stalinism, and a source, no doubt, of differends and of the vengeance that hovers about that particular name. But if the repressiveness of this mechanism stems from its inability to articulate differences within it, is this purely and simply the result of an equivalential logic gone too far—or, not far enough? The *communism* of the communist enumeration can be guaranteed only if each member of the co-alition can name itself and be named as difference within the commonality of their differences, if each addressee and referent can also have its turn as addres-sor. There is no relation of equivalence unless the egalitarian demand of *commu-n*ism is met. It is not met when a meta-instance bureaucratically arrogates to it-self the right to speak for all and as all, and hence asserts an explicit or concealed autonomy (or self-naming) that is precisely the *end* of democratic equivalence and the institution of new inequities.

The "expansive logic of equivalences" has also been repeatedly checked in another way ever since the Stalinist retrenchment of socialism "within one coun-try" and the rise of movements in quest of specifically *national* liberation— checked, that is, by the geopolitical limits of the nation-state, whether its fron-tiers be the legacy of imperialist convenience or of bourgeois revolution. In these cases, the phrasing of national unity as such runs the risk of a reactionary col-lapse back onto the localized names and traditional narratives of a nation con-ceived in its exclusivity from all others. As Lyotard warns on the very last page of *The Differend*, "Proud struggles for independence end in young, reactionary States" (no. 262). At the other extreme would be the cosmopolitan or "great" narrative that imperialistically subsumes all particular names under a universal one. This pessimistic alternative, adumbrated near the end of Lyotard's book (nos. 221–35), phrases the problem of the international community (and no thought of community is valid unless it can also rise to the global level) according to the same dilemma we have already noted between an immanence of the whole subtending the parts and an immanence of the parts unto themselves. To pursue the direction indicated by Nancy, reflection on this question must begin from the difficulty of thinking the relation, here international relations, as inaugural. In terms of the name, the issue is not the alternative between respecting the name in its particularity, on the one hand, and subsuming it into a universalizing history, on the other. As Lyotard would be the first to argue, the issue is not the name, but rather *how to link onto* the name in a way that responsibly challenges the contingency of its sense(s).

As such, it should be noted that contemporaneous with the rise of the "new social movements" discussed by Laclau and Mouffe, new and unprecedented possibilities have arisen for the articulation of equivalences that form hegemonic blocs *transnationally*. This seems to me, in fact, to be one of the most important and least understood of the legacies left by the sixties, in particular the Vietnam War, as fought not along a traditional front but in and around a dispersed set of positions, of place-*names*, reaching from Indochinese jungles to American university campuses, its guerrilla actions spilling over frontiers in ways that betrayed solidarities across national lines, thus questioning the traditional labeling of patriot and traitor. Today, for example, struggles by and in solidarity with the peoples of Central America or southern Africa have little to do with the sovereignty of national frontiers, and the attempt to phrase such struggles within the existing framework of international legality is often misguided or dangerously regressive to the extent that it upholds the geopolitical status quo and easily risks an essentialist view of the nation. The violent perniciousness of such an essentialism, typified by the politics of blood and soil that refuses all humanity to "outsiders," has repeatedly been demonstrated in this century. In fact, it is at this very point that we rejoin the differends discussed earlier concerning various "dispossessed" ethnicities, for while autonomy may be a necessary goal, it is hardly a sufficient one: the self-naming of the name (auto-nomy) is but *one* way of phrasing it, one that can easily neglect the urgency and difficulty of linking it onto other names and within other phrases. The necessity of what Lyotard, after Kant, calls a "cosmo-political" point of view (*Differend*, no. 217), which would *critically*—that is, differentially—articulate particular names within a radically democratic *and internationalist* politics, is also the possibility of a hegemonic rejoinder to that most recent and insidious phase of capitalism, multinationalism, which, as Lyotard notes, already well understands the value of a play between equivalence and autonomy in its urgent need to establish new markets (*Differend*, no. 255).

Likewise, the struggle, adumbrated by Laclau and Mouffe in the final pages of *Hegemony and Socialist Strategy*, to reappropriate and redefine the "*meaning of liberal discourse*" (176) in the wake of its appropriation by the New Right should not forget also to reclaim those words disparaged by the same forces. Thus, alongside the discursive repossession of terms such as liberty, equality, justice, and democracy, shouldn't we also think about rearticulating the word communism by stepping over and beyond its current affects of either diminished hopes or preternatural dread (at least, in a post-1950s American context) and by listening to what as yet remains unheard or smothered under this concept-name that once energetically mobilized the "enthusiasm of peoples" (to quote Kant's phrase about the French Revolution ["An Old Question," 144]), and that remains stilled, as Sartre noted already long ago in *Questions de méthode* (24–32), even by the theoretical purity of an academic Marxism (not the same name!) that often views "communism" with embarrassment as the failure of practice?

Is it possible, in other words, and at the risk perhaps of offending *our* deconstructive sensibilities, to "breathe new life" into that old specter that, in Marx's famous line (*Communist Manifesto*, 6), once haunted Europe and that continues somewhere, somehow, to *haunt* us today, well after its time and in an age when so-called communism offers but a ghost image of its former self, one whose materiality seems to vanish into insubstantiality upon closer inspection?

What is communism, though, if not a call for equality that foregrounds issues of social value and worth on a terrain not covered by the merely political "rights" of democratic liberalism? Can this communism not be radicalized by extending its appeal beyond the rectification of the (very real!) exploitation in the workplace to include, at the very least, a comparable critique of exploitative relations in the field of the symbolic economy with its capitalization of cultural "value," and beyond that for an end to all inequities whatsoever, wherever they may be found? As such, communism would be formulated perhaps less as a political project than as an ethical demand or imperative. It is, if you like, and as numerous attempts at communism have shown, a call that can never be *fully* answered. Just as the name has no final sense, or history a predetermined end, so there will always be inequalities and injustices to be righted. There is not and cannot ever be a purely communistic state. Perhaps this is the sense of Maurice Blanchot's remark about communism that it is "what excludes (and is excluded by) every already constituted community" (32; cited in Nancy, *La Communauté désoeuvrée*, 25). The revolution can only be betrayed by the irrepressible rise of new social stratifications, antagonisms, and differends, but this is no argument against political action, even revolution, *so long as* we understand communism as naming what Lyotard calls, after Kant, an "Idea of reason." Belonging to practical reason, such an Idea is conceivable but never presentable: "It is a sort of horizon that performs a regulatory role with respect to action" (*Just Gaming*, 46). As an Idea, communism is the name of an egalitarian horizon, not the "insuperable" one of our time, but one to which we can never fully accede. Communism is irretrievably over (or under) the horizon, what orients obscurely and from afar an ethics of radical egalitarianism that is ever, but never solely, critical. Incapable of ever being fully actualized, like the Kantian community of the aesthetic judgment (cf. Lyotard, *Peregrinations*, 38), the ghost of communism names something "intractable" or "unmanageable" (Lyotard in this volume; Blanchot, 32) that no community can ever treat, manage, or conjure away to the extent that it irrepressibly returns to haunt that community by the urgency of its call (irredeemably *utopic* in character)[3] for egalitarianism with regard to all rights, privileges, and properties (including symbolic capital), and at its limit, the equality of sharing what cannot be shared, the incommunicable community of our finitudes (to speak the language of Nancy). Hence, its vengeance, which, to answer our initial reprise of Lyotard's eminently rhetorical question, can only be: *forever*.

If, as Blanchot writes citing Lenin, the "soul" of communism lies precisely in "what makes it *intolerable, intractable, unmanageable* [ce qui le rend *intolérable, intraitable*]" (32), then rather than a ghost whose intractableness needs to be laid to rest (by repression or even by litigation), the liminality of communism is a differend perpetually to be renewed, so as, at the very least, in the words that close *The Postmodern Condition*, to "save the honor of the name" (82).

Notes

1. The example of journalism is, of course, not an idle one. Nor is it even simply an example in the context of the polemics surrounding the surfacing of de Man's "wartime writings," for the ethics of journalism as a public discourse is the very matter of the argument not only with regard to de Man's contributions to Belgian newspapers from 1940 to 1942, but also with regard to the way the recent "discovery" of those texts has been presented by contemporary American and European journalists. The theme of journalism is also very much at the heart of Jacques Derrida's long essay, "Paul de Man's War" (*Critical Inquiry* 14 [1988], 590–652).

2. As Richard Terdiman points out in his contribution to this volume, Nancy misquotes or "misremembers" Sartre's statement in the preface to the *Critique de la raison dialectique* (Paris: Gallimard, 1960), 9, which refers not to communism as such but to "Marxism" as a philosophy, a move crucial to Sartre's justification for a Marxian existentialism that is independent and distinct from what he sees as the reified, formalized, and doctrinal thinking of the "official" Marxism spoken by intellectuals publicly affiliated with the Communist movement. In any case, Nancy's "mistake" notwithstanding, his ensuing remark about the "disappearance, impossibility, or condemnation of communism" as the "new insuperable horizon" seems difficult to contest in the wake of a cold war ideology that has distinguished between a "bad" or "flawed" communist world and a "good" or still recuperable Marxist theory, a distinction that seems to be universally held, in the West at least, by left, right, and liberal alike. In place of the utopic dream (or dread) of worldwide Communist revolution that reigned in the mid-twentieth century, current discourse about the "demise" of communism seems to pervade political thinking of all persuasions as an unquestioned *presupposition* that indeed turns it into the (very questionable) horizon from which the political is thought today.

3. I use the term "utopic" in the precise sense attributed to it by Louis Marin in *Utopiques: jeux d'espaces* (Paris: Minuit, 1973), for whom it designates a radical and resolutely critical *practice* of fiction that, on the one hand, "neutralizes" the bipolarity of an ideological construction to reveal its constitutive gaps and contradictions. On the other hand, the irrepressibly concomitant formation of a "utopia" as a theoretical model that exhausts the social cannot help but resuture the exposed gaps and contradictions into a new ideological form, into a "utopian" *myth* legitimating new forms of social oppression. On this same problem, also see Fredric Jameson's "Of Islands and Trenches: Neutralization and the Production of Utopian Discourse" (*Diacritics*, 7 [1977], 2–21).

A l'insu
(Unbeknownst)

Jean-François Lyotard

If we had time—but that's the whole point, *we don't have the time* (after a certain age, this is well known; whereas earlier, we believe we have time; to grow older is to learn that we will not have had the time; and Europe is old, face-liftings notwithstanding)—if we had time, we would seize the opportunity afforded by subjects like "The Politics of Forgetting" or "May '68: Twenty Years Later" to make a point by taking stock of where we are (*faire le point*). An illusory wish, and necessarily so. Points are marked out in space—in the middle of the ocean or in vast deserts—to which coordinate measurements are applied. But there are no points in time. We cannot even claim to be located in the immensity of time. Time discourages the attempt to "co-ordinate" and the hope of "locating ourselves."

In wanting to "mark out our point" (*faire le point*) we are already going astray. We are already forgetting what time is. Or rather, through the subterfuge of the spatial metaphor, time allows itself to be forgotten. Physicists have understood this, but not the rest of us humans.

It would not be a point, but on the contrary a universal proposition that we could make, one affirmed from every possible point: namely, that all politics is a politics of forgetting, and that nonforgetting (which is not memory) eludes politics.

I am not speaking of something that we could attribute to politics itself, of an intention to make forgotten. Intention has nothing at all to do with it. It's rather a question of "short-term memory," of that temporal disposition included in the rules governing a civil or citizenly community of whatever kind, and which requires that something in it be forgotten. What we could say is that what is forgotten, of course, is that this community remains intractable (*intraitable*) to the treatment of political unity; or again, that this treatment has in appearance to be renewed "from time to time," while in reality it has to be renewed all the time, perpetually. What cannot be treated, what is not manageable [*traitable*] once and for all, and what is forgotten by political treatment in its constitution of a "commonality" of humans by dint of their belonging to the same polis, is the very thing that is not shareable among them, what is not communicable or communal or common at all. Call it birth and/or death, or even singularity. On this, see Jean-Luc Nancy's *Inoperative Community*.

Here, I do not wish to conjure up some kind of aggressiveness, death drive, or death struggle among humans that are whole, constituted, and organized into sects, parties, or movements. Nor even organized into individualities who rebel against any kind of association. It is the business of politics to make that sort of separation *its* business. Politics never ceases calling for union, for solidarity; and, in the least bad of cases, it turns the manner of being together into the object of an open-ended negotiation, the object of a better-distributed justice or of a consultation that remains to be pursued. This daily fare of politics is not an easy matter. It is the art of Machiavelli. And ever since the authority of partitioning and sharing (*partage*) was denied "real presence" after and by the execution of Louis XVI, we know that the so-called democratic debate not only bears upon possessions (economic, moral, intellectual) to be divided, upon rights to be affirmed and taken into account in deliberation and distribution, but that the debate also, inclusively, bears upon the authority that governs the debate and, sometimes, even upon the very principle of the debate, at the constitutional level.

That is what was exposed in its horror when old Europe suffered its "crisis" during the era of totalitarianisms. Aside from that horror, there remains the striking fact, noted by Hannah Arendt and Franz Neumann, that the totalitarian apparatus, constituted as a result of the elimination of debate and by the continuous elimination of debate from political life by means of terror, reproduces within itself, in the anatomy and physiology of its national body politic, the illness that it claims to cure. Disorder within, an internal proliferation of decision-making authorities, war among inner-circle cliques: all this betrays the recurrence of the shameful sickness within what passes for health and betrays the "presence" of the unmanageable (*intraitable*), at the very time that the latter is hidden away by the delirium and arrogance of a unitary, totalitarian politics.

Betraying the unmanageable, these factors manifest it anew while reversing its meaning, and indeed by the very fact of reversing its meaning. Shiny, jack-booted rigidity is like the obverse of a poorly circumscribed thing that "inhabits" society without even being felt. With the horror resulting from this sanitizing operation, the phantasm of oneness and totality is sustained by the belief that this heterogeneous thing has, or is, a face (Medusa's face?), and that it would suffice to turn it around to get rid of it. And indeed, it is endowed with a face, with a name, a representation (''the jews,'' for example)[1] wherein is invested everything that is supposed to be contrary to the distinctness—and inauspicious for the health—of the social body. But precisely, the thing has no more of a reverse side than it has a right side, it has no place, not having taken place and being ''present'' only outside representation: in death, in birth, one's absolute and singular dependency, which prohibits any instantiated disposition of oneself from being unitary and total. I could just as well say ''sexual difference,'' in the most radical sense of a heteronomy that does not belong to the space-time of representation. That is why it can hardly be felt in the ''soul of the polis.''

It is felt, in the sense that it is not heard or seen. It is not represented either by words or by ''things'' (images), as Freud used to say. Freud also designated its mode of ''presence'' by using the senseless expression: ''unconscious affect.'' It has nothing to do with the imaginary nor, consequently—looking at the thing socially—with ideology. I leave to Nicole Loraux, whose theses I am approaching here, the question of whether it is permissible to envision the thing socially. In my opinion, there is no doubt about it, but I understand that historians resist the hypothesis that the polis has a soul, and that one must therefore disarm their defenses. No doubt there is *some soul* at stake in the polis, if by ''soul'' we mean the part of spirit that remains hostage to the thing, that remains susceptible to anguish, and defenseless. Historians, after all, are also trying to build a polis, and they strive, or lend themselves, to forgetting that affect.

What is essential to the unmanageable thing is that it absolutely must be gotten rid of. It can be approached only as the unbearable, the repulsive. Its way of attracting is to repulse. At least, that is what the mind recounts about it when it obeys the ancient call of the *logos* (the conceiving function) to corral, to determine, to expose and articulate everything—even the untimely thing—as an object. For, as far as the mind's clandestine passenger is concerned, we can and must suppose that it does not enter into the economic and dynamic game of attractions and repulsions, and that it is not waiting for us to concern ourselves with it or to ''redeem'' it by intelligence. It is what ''occupies'' the mind while disabling it. This occupation solicits a kind of paranoia. The ''discontent of civilization,'' the sharp and vague feeling that the civilians are not civilized and that something is ill-disposed toward civility, all this easily engenders the suspicion that plots are being hatched. Also easily engendered are trials, the denunciation of scapegoats, the exclusion of the *xenos*, the accusations made against opposing parties, slander, eristics. And the revolutionary idea, too. *Polemos* is not the father of all things, he is the child of this relation of the mind to a thing that has no relation to the mind. And *polemos* too is a way for the mind to forget it, to forget the *coitus impossibilis* that engendered it and never stops engendering it.

If the thing is not manageable politically, it is because it is outside the chain. If we seek to link it onto the chain, which is the whole business of politics, it remains unlinked and only inspires yet more unleashing. Revolutions, all revolutions, are attempts to approach it, to make the community more faithful to what, unbeknownst to it, inhabits it; at the same time, revolutions attempt to regulate, to suppress, to efface the effects that the thing engenders. There is a fidelity and an infidelity in the fact of revolution. An attentiveness to what "is not working," a voice and an ear lent to a grave wrong done to the community, whatever that wrong may be called. Marx, for example, revealed its cause, or so he believed, in the exploitation of labor power, in the sacrifice of pure creative power that results from the capitalist organization of being together. I say "pure" creative power, because Marx endows it with an attribute that no mechanism of exchange possesses (be it chemical, physical, or human), namely, the property of expending or consuming *less* energy (less value) than it produces as it goes into action (into productive action, that is, as it goes to work). Thus, this power must be unleashed from the chains that bind it in the intrigue of the contract and on the stage of the market. It must be unbound from the *pseudon* (contract, work, average social time required) in which it is preferred, imagined, exposed, betrayed. Revolution, according to Marx, clearly means this fidelity to the non-enchained.

It seems to me that May '68 was marked by such a fidelity. From the outset, the unleashing expanded to culture. May '68 was faithful to the thing that would suffer from its being represented and directed toward the civil sector, the thing that would therefore be ill-treated, not only in the factory or the office, but also at school, and throughout the "cultural" institution (which became manifest at that time and which today we encounter everywhere, including here).[2] And, of course, this thing would also have been ill-treated in political life itself. In the streets of France, the thing was supposedly exposed live—at the cost, of course, of a thousand ideologies of the most contradictory kind. But this very incoherence in the representations can be chalked up to a kind of fidelity, which it served to guarantee. The question of political power was hardly asked, in the final analysis. When, in late May and June, it did get asked by the left, extreme or not, on the rostrum and at work, when the political parties began once again to bark up a storm, the thing fell silent, if indeed it had ever spoken, or even heaved a sigh. The effects of the unleashing persisted, but in the guise of traces. Like any memory, although sometimes in the very name of fidelity, the function of these traces was always to help forget the threat that everyone, whether in the movement or against it (always both at the same time, no doubt), had experienced. One strives to become a realist, an activist, either stupidly or intelligently. By "intelligently" I mean with the Machiavellian intelligence that is aware at least that politics cannot avoid betraying the thing. In any case, realism requires amnesia.

Thus it is that the success of revolutions is necessarily their failure, and that their infidelity is produced out of the very "exploit" or exploitation of their fidelity. On the political "score card" (at once disastrous and illuminating) that, unbeknownst to it, the century coming to an end is mentally tallying up, a question arises: are there other politics—other than revolutionary—that would make it possible not to be unfaithful to the thing that inhabits the polis unconsciously?

But how could such a goal be achieved by a politics, when politics is already devoted to the scene of representation from which the unpresentable presumably must be eliminated, unless politics is to risk losing the polis? The very manner of speaking about forgetting here, I realize, makes no political sense. Only a sense of melancholy. While giving up on revolution, we still cannot finish mourning for this fidelity, even though, and above all because, we know it to be impossible. Politics will never be anything but the art of the possible.

In this state of affairs, recourse to human rights brings slight consolation. Human rights define only the limits that public power ought not to cross. They can do no more than to prohibit public power from unleashing the polis, in the way that all legal entities are limited. Human rights must be respected like a clear memory and a clear-sightedness, the memory of itself that the republic must conserve if it does not wish to fall into ruin. Human rights, then, are defensive. They are defense mechanisms against the nonlinked, and as a citizen, one has the duty to interiorize them and to put them to work in public situations, to direct them to all others, oneself included. As such, human rights are one of the ways to forget: to forget that, in every mind and in the ensemble of minds that is the republican community, there is something which has no rights that need to be affirmed, but which, beyond the just and the unjust, exceeds the mind of each and all. In the republican principle, man and his autonomy come to scramble, under the guise of laws and rights, the traces of an immemorial dependency.

"Resistance" can be used in two senses. Rights resist the thing, and the thing resists rights. Clear memory resists the immemorial that threatens it, derails it, wears it down like the clouds of matter that can slow the course of photons approaching from far away. It is in this way that our present relation to the idea of Enlightenment is altered by the thickness of a night. Elie Wiesel's *Night*. And you can't escape this aporia by adding memory to the list of human rights. If one had to situate the respect due the thing in the doctrine of justice, one would be obliged to count it among the duties rather than among the rights. It is the debt, par excellence. But, yet again, the thing does not belong to a doctrine, it expects and requires nothing from the mind, it exceeds all prescription—even all permission—of an institutional nature. If, unbeknownst to it, the mind is indebted to the thing, it is not because the thing has been contractually instituted as the mind's creditor following a request for a loan. The mind will have been dispossessed "before" being able to certify or to act as a subject. It is consigned to the unending effort to repossess itself over and against the thing, which means, to forget it. This thing will turn out always to have been the mind's childhood, this enigma that the mind existed ''before'' existing.

The events of May '68 — once shorn of its hodgepodge of intentions, wills, strategies, and conciliatory illusions — took on their luster, an intelligible luster, really, from what they revealed of childhood. I do not mean that the movement was motivated and carried along by a collective infantile regression, nor even that the majority of those swept up in it obviously were young people. I mean that May '68 clearly showed a scrupulous fidelity to a state of dependency more immanent to the mind than its state of mind. This state of dependency was, I repeat, an unbearable one, and we were protesting against it without being able to name the ''cause,'' the thing, *la cosa* (indeed unnamable). But at the same time, it was an admirable state that we insisted deserved homage, as if we could in that way get the civil community (the adult community) to recognize that, despite its ideals of autonomy and progress (or because of them), such a community could not avoid leaving a residue beyond its control, to which the community itself remained hostage, unbeknownst to it.

The return to order that all the political parties prescribed in different styles but with a single voice, from the extreme left to the right, was quite simply an urgent request to forget this thing — childhood. The Marxisms, from the more radical Workers' Council movement to the less radical Maoism, had their part, a decisive part, in occulting what was being revealed — or rather what was showing itself. Each in its own way rendered the thing manageable once again by inscribing it within the register of political perspectives, including that of ''splinter-group activism,'' the supreme nonsense, or countersense, with regard to the thing.

In the West at least, in the West of politics and metaphysics, any revelation is for the mind the event, perhaps, of a greater proximity to the forgotten-unforgettable thing, which leaves it disabled. The event of 1968 — ''les événements,'' as we have since called it in France — is remarkable for the anguish it taps. In the mind, childhood is not happiness and innocence, but the state of dependency. Childhood itself seeks to rid itself of that state and to become ''grown-up.'' It does not give evidence of its irresponsibility as a self-flattery, but as a complaint. May '68 sighed the lament of an incurable suffering, the suffering of not having been born free. This lament returned in an immense echo. Like a tragic chorus, adults lamented the lament of child heroes.

And yet, May '68 was not a tragedy; there was no dénouement, no crime, and if blood was spilled it was not the doing of the enraged children. They were not fulfilling a destiny inflicted on them by an oracle requiring their life's passion. Its representation as tragedy itself seemed, no less than politics, still *too* unfaithful to the thing. May '68 was not a revolution, because its actors were just young enough or old enough, just aware enough of the status of the polis, to know instinctively that today politics can in no way be tragedy. They knew that tragical-political terror is only an effect, and that horror (its true name) *repeats* the immemorial terror in which the mind has been dispossessed. They did everything they possibly could to avoid this repetition. They did not want, in their acts, to repeat the terror, born of the thing, but to invoke it through their gesture, as poets.

Since it was not revolutionary, the movement of May '68 was not destined to fall into unfaithfulness. Once the "demonstration" had shown that all politics is a politics of forgetting, it remained such as it was in our minds, serious and inconsistent, even as our minds forgot it. "Les événements" became *unheimlich*, both strange and familiar, like the thing to which they had given witness. Their innumerable "effects" (school, sex, woman, family, work, etc.) came to be inscribed not as effects of '68, but rather as new initiatives in ordinary political and civil life. The West went back to its work of managing the unmanageable (*traitement de l'intraitable*).

Translated by James Creech and
Georges Van Den Abbeele

Notes

1. See my *Heidegger and "the jews,"* trans. Andreas Michel and Mark S. Roberts (Minneapolis: University of Minnesota Press, 1990), 3, for an explanation of my use of quotation marks and lower case for "the jews."

2. By "here," Lyotard refers specifically to the colloquium at which this paper was read and generally to the "cultural institution" manifested by the contemporary scholarly conference. — Ed.

Communal Crisis

Verena Andermatt Conley

From the solitude of the North Woods, I am led to wonder what it means to med-
itate on our chosen topic of community. My library here is in keeping with my
surroundings: *Wildflowers of North America*, *Our Birds*, and *The Edible Mush-
room*, volumes that will inflect somewhat, I hope, the words to follow. The book
on mushrooms features glossy reproductions of the exquisite morel, whose
name—when pronounced with a little French inflection—is not without echoes
of the philosophers' moral law. In a guide to the study of boreal trees, I learn
about their communities with divisions into canopies and subcanopies. The basic
organizing principle of trees appears to be the search for food. To obtain the latter, action is decisive, often violent, and quite a contrast with the point of departure for the very colloquium that puts into question a community working along
such lines of inclusion, exclusion.

A word about this book title. Last year, in preparation for Jean-François Lyotard's visit at Miami University, each of us submitted a question. Mine had to do
with the status of the intellectual in the present-day world and with certain inevitable contradictions I perceived. After reading my question, Tom Conley said to
me: "Mais quand-même, you should not ask questions like this, ad hominem."
Somewhat contrite, I went to apologize to Jean-François Lyotard, who said in his
cultivated, urbane style, with resonances of an Eastern sage, "Oh, I just read in
your question that you were in crisis." "In crisis," the words echoed in my
head, "in crisis." Surely it was not that famous forty-year-old crisis, the cliché
so dear to some of our administrators that helps them to settle complex issues by
draconian means. Thinking about what had been called "my crisis," I discov-

49

ered that it was not a *toujours déjà*, an always already, but that it could be attributed to be moment and a place. Something had been determined by my return to
Miami University last fall with a change in my life that, due to a regular schedule
of commuting, took me out of a serene campus community, built on the nine-
teeth-century agrarian model, and plunged me into a world of airports, airplanes,
and electronics. What struck me was not only that the world that was hustling and

bustling was totally ignorant of my ways of reading and did not seem to care, but that what I was discovering seemed to be what in fact made the world go round. This world was quite different from the one I had been proposing in my courses and in my writings—based mainly on a reading of French feminist theories, in which a breakdown of community, an unavowable community, an undoing of the self in a discourse of intense poetic vision was in question. These discourses had

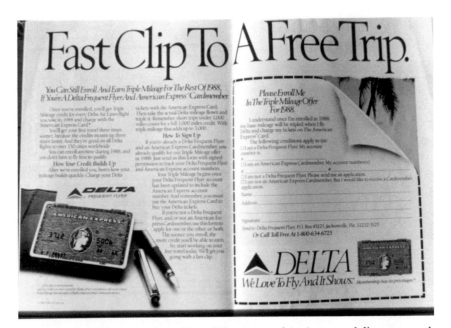

taught me about dispossession, about *délivrance* and *jouissance*, deliverance and pleasure, about politics through poetry. I seemed to have gone from one flight to another, from one delta to another; from Hélène Cixous's textual machines, always in flight, alighting here and there at nodal points, and Marguerite Duras's haunting deltas that no barrage can control, to what was called, in a condensation of the two, postmodern travel by Delta Airlines. And as everybody knows, they say, "Delta loves to fly and it shows." Now, what is it like to fly Delta and read the world? If the series of weekly displacements erases an old sense of communal bonding tied to a place in which one lives, loves, and toils, my new experience is not devoid of newly proclaimed communal bondings. By "choosing Delta"—note the freedom implicit in the American way of life where, contrary to the European, no state machine dares interfere—I enter into a complex network of micro- and macrocommunities (or commutities, the difference being that of a *t*), all seemingly quite avowable. Language is plain and all allegiance is based on saving time and money. Through a communal bonding between Delta and Amexco, I earn triple mileage on my Frequent Flyer Card (the mileage statement is courteously sent each month to "Mr. Vern Conley"), enough to pay for a trip for two next year to the Orient—not to the exotic Parisian China of Kristeva's erstwhile Taji-quan, but to Tokyo. My Crown card gives me access to The Club, where businessmen are tied to the world via long-distance calling cards—rather than the feminist *téléfaune*—or conducting conferences in special seminar rooms at the airport. It is the twentieth-century version of the first floor of the Eiffel

Tower, which was supposed to be a futuristic world of its own. Only academics have the luxury of traveling fifty miles from the airport to a conference — have the time to spend, surely not the money. In the Club, the barman says hello, and so does the community of regulars, set apart from the tourists waiting for their flight to London. Delta effectively provides you with a home away from home. Or rather, Delta becomes the home, in displacement, held together by a mutual interest in gain. Businessmen, the beatniks of the eighties, are "on the road." In flight, everything is done to do away with that sensation. A continuous flow of liquid prevents the passengers from acceding to the sublime: there is no jolt, no stopping followed by a flow. *Sky* magazine, put at the disposal of the community of flyers — mostly men — offers a reading of the world based on straight materialism, optimal gain, and a direct rapport between name and referent. A world of market research, efficiency, and reasoning projects the future. There are glossy ads for electronic gadgets, from worldwide pagers to Panasonic VCRs with remote control to videodiscs that tell doctors whether they are right or wrong and computers that translate into different languages. The monthly psychological column in September of 1987 informed the reader of the effects of therapy: chemical therapy is the best for those who need it. Freudian therapy also works but is slower. One month's time is gained by using A rather than B. All is done to save time, to eliminate human error, and ultimately to save money. The new configuration is linked to new supersubjects, as exemplified by the world of SyberVision. If I choose to enter the world of SyberVision (conveniently accessible with an 800 number and all major credit cards), I can listen by way of tapes and cassettes to melodious, paternal voices, reciting texts by eminent professors of management from USC and Stanford University, or to sports figures like Jean-Claude Killy, who guarantee to change my life in every area of my choice, from leadership to high achievement, from executive stress to a better marriage, from an improved golf game to weight control. As with the trees I am watching while I am writing this, there are communities and subcommunities everywhere — perhaps, like the white pines, spraying their acid on intruders. SyberVision is yet another community of men and women, based on the assumption of a common language, where, like the image of the muscular couple advertising the program, its users are "in charge." It guarantees the American version of success defined by eternal youth, good looks, and money. The ultimate in the development of any philosophy of the subject and mastery of the self, SyberVision is perhaps best allegorized by the ad for the program on self-discipline, featuring the mountain from my erstwhile homeland, the Matterhorn, surmounted by a dollar sign. What Jean-François Lyotard called my crisis had to do with my becoming aware, all at once, of the gap between my feminist discourses, those that seemingly made the world go round, and the distance covered from the days of Vietnam to the present days of "yuppie ennui"; between the days when Patti Hearst was a member of the Symbionese Liberation Army and those during which, as a New York socialite, she presented the film Paul Schrader made about her to the Cannes Film Festival; between what I entered in my twenties as critical and tactical

avant-garde discourses, which proposed to change, artistically and theoretically, modes of production and reproduction, and a world that, at many levels, has developed in disregard of them. Lyotard's final invitation in *The Differend* to listen to the unpresentable — *'Arrive-t-il,''* Is it happening? — was here supplanted by the ultimate in market research.[1]

I had come to this country nourished by romantic, filmic images from *Gone*

with the Wind and *Geronimo*, with clichéd readings about the Far West by Karl May. But I had found the Living Theater in teargassed streets in Madison, Wisconsin, which made me decide to leave the statues of the reformers in the courtyard at Geneva far behind. It is from there that I had entered feminist discourses, Cixous's undoing of the narcissistic *sujet un*, Kristeva's revolution through poetic language, Irigaray's doubling of the woman, or Wittig's assimilation of the woman's cause with that of the flower children. Feminist writings, vaguely

linked to the German romantics, to the literary absolute, to the integration of otherness in reason, and to Freudian models of repression, urged for the unleashing of potentially creative forces. I had been trained to view art as subversive, emancipatory, and ultimately reconciling. But these discourses seemed to have been overwhelmed by those I found in the back pockets of the seats on Delta Airlines.

The question became, like that phrased by Lyotard, though in a different context, how to link: "*Comment enchaîner?*"

After reading recent publications, I concluded that the "crisis" wasn't mine alone. There seems to be a more general malaise with a world dominated by the *genre économique*, run by large, almost anonymous corporations, or communities, broken down into myriad smaller ones, and with theories that—after an ephemeral moment of '68—did not bring about the proposed universal changes, be it through a historical genealogy, the temporalization of the origin, or a reading of the world in terms of language games. It seemed less like a community at loose ends than a loose-ended community at loose ends.

This I gathered from various calls to action: Paul Smith's book *Discerning the Subject*; Jürgen Habermas's *Philosophische Diskurs der Moderne: 12 Vorlesungen*, an attempt at critically historicizing contemporary discourses, deftly translated into French but a bit narrowly introduced by Christian Bouchindhomme and Rainer Rochlitz; an issue of *Diacritics* (17, 3 [Fall 1987]) featuring articles urging a return to history (a subject that had never really disappeared) and exhorting the reader to be both "affirmative and contestatory"; as well as a review by David B. Downing of Christopher Norris's new "politics of enlightened critique," which alternates between Lyotard and Habermas and opts for Fregean logical semantics.[2] Downing, with perspicacity, focuses on the disagreement between Lyotard and Habermas. Lyotard insists on locating any form of emancipatory rhetoric as dependent on one of the great metanarratives of Western culture. He privileges the gap or rupture as a departure for the new, the unheard, the unpresentable. Habermas attempts to link theory with pragmatics through his three categories of knowledge: technical, practical, and emancipatory, and insists on making abstract theory point to specific counterdominant political movements such as those of peace, ecology, and feminism. (*Communicative Action*, 35, 73). Their differend, as Thomas McCarthy points out in his introduction to *The Theory of Communicative Action*,[3] seems to revolve around a question of linking, of a playful twentieth-century aesthetics, insisting on the unpresentable, from Duchamp's readymade to the linguistic configurations of the new novel, versus a linking of abstract theory to a more pragmatic field. And, concludes Downing, in favor of Habermas against Norris's reading of Frege and leaving aside Lyotard: "This perhaps will allow us to make headway in questions of inequality, of race, class, gender." The emancipatory discourse prevails. Only hinted at, but not taken up again, are, next to feminism, questions of ecology and peace. This all reads as a part of the intellectual's desire to act in and on a world that eludes him, and I choose *him* purposely because the women's theoretical preoccupations seem to be less exteriorized, less regulatory, in accord with a tradition of gender—or perhaps a wisdom to be cultivated?

There also arrived two issues of *Critique*, one featuring an article on "the invasion of French theory in America" (April 1988, 491), and the other on philosophy, on "how it continues" (June–July 1988, 493–94). The former title may confirm that malaise is worldwide, that America looks to European theory for issues that it cannot solve and Europe to American pragmatism. A point about invasion, since I am meditating on this in the North Woods, between Belgium Fred's and the DeCaigny Rapids: the very idea of "invasion" may be an American interpretation of French behavior. The famous voyageurs, traveling after the Greenwich meridian had already replaced that of Paris on the Picard map, were not invaders; they were interested in local exchange among riverain Indian groups, in trading copper pots and trinkets for beaver pelts. They found in America some ideal communities, be it that of the beavers, the *castor gras* (reproduced with quasi-human physiognomies in the style of Fontainebleau), or their version of a first Disneyland, an Indian community of 1552 set up for the king's enjoyment in Rouen. The French seemed more interested in how the world was constituted than in changing it for colonial ends.

What I sense from all these readings is a malaise concerning our discourses, our positions in the world—or perhaps an attempt to make an evaluation, à la Dumas, twenty years later: "self-criticism, action, contestation" are the terms. Yet the general climate in America is not good. Bouchindhomme and Rochlitz quite sincerely refer to a world about to become extinct. This may be true. But it certainly is not lived that way by many, and there's the rub.

Following the debacle of the Communist party in France, roughly twenty years after World War II and its leading role in the Resistance, Hélène Cixous was able to say in an interview printed in the party's cultural review *Les Lettres françaises*: "Politically, there has been a move to the left, an effraction of what used to be called 'leftist' and constituted a large part of the traditional public: liberals, intellectuals, humanists, academics are retreating and are on the defensive in relation to an avant-garde production that does not allow them any subjective gratification and undermines their values. Inversely, there has been a breakthrough: a public of young people now has access to what an authoritarian, test-oriented university discourse did not allow even three or four years ago. What is being read at Vincennes is unreadable in other universities in stagnation."[4]

After World War II and the Algerian War, May '68 certainly seemed a rallying point for many. It seemed to be a time in France when changes in production and reproduction could be brought about, when the community was to open onto a communism based on love without an object. The revolution of poetic language was going to lead to the promised land, via the conscience of women, workers, Jews, and China. The Vietnam War seemed to rally Americans and orient them in a direction in accord with these discourses.

But things developed differently. A certain form of capitalism, if we may still call it that, seems at an all-time high. Economic interests dominate political interests. *Le genre économique*, as Lyotard would have it, is all-pervasive, making every linking or *enchaînement* conflictual, in philosophers' terms, or in managerial terms, aggressive and hostile. We may begin to wonder whether terms like left and right, residues of the French Revolution, still apply, whether other ways of designating should be thought of, away from a certain ideal of emancipation to something more communally prescriptive—as when we worry, for example, about the rain forests being depleted, for how are we going "to swim in air," as the feminists exhort us, when there is no more air to swim in? Colbert, though his project was economically controversial, in the mid-seventeenth century planted an oak forest near Charroux in Auvergne for wood to be cut in 1990 to rebuild the French navy. Today, foresight is at an all-time low, and people seem to live entirely for the profit of the day. Gallup polls show, for the presidential election in November, more women than men are ready to vote for Democrats, and more people over fifty than between the ages of eighteen and twenty-four. It is the young people who plan to vote Republican—that is, loosely, to the right. The yuppies (or the dinks) are far from that *public de jeunes* (a public of young people) acclaimed by Hélène Cixous in 1968. However, more college graduates than nongraduates will vote for the Democrats—marking, ever so remotely, an interest in social issues.

Perhaps we should situate ourselves, redefine ourselves as trading in French theories in America today, be it as voyageurs, as settlers, or as natives. An attempt at linking heterogeneous discourses cannot be made without an evaluation of a rapidly changing position of the thinker and the artist in the world. And who is the communal ''we''? Lyotard thinks of himself as a philosopher, as someone analyzing how the world is constituted. He distinguishes himself agonistically from the intellectuals, whom he sees as noisily rallying around a cause without any sign of rigorous analysis. The philosopher, taking his models from the world he analyzes—at times a French world—is to be both in the world and above it, showing how it is constituted. I am not a philosopher and have no debt to pay. But having been trained in reading literature and film, I have always taken it upon myself to read the world critically through these media. What is the relationship between the world and art, how does a certain piece less reflect than predict and criticize by opening onto something new? Like Lyotard, I situate myself in an aesthetic of discontinuity, in a tradition favoring social change through art, without attaching to it the present negativizing label of aestheticism. This is all perhaps in keeping with the preponderant role of art since the German romantics, echoed for literary people in Freud's dictum that ''poets are ahead of us common men,'' and with the potentially revolutionizing capabilities of art that underlie a lot of French theories being questioned. Perhaps we ought to situate ourselves and see what we are trying to achieve. ''We'' here are a ''community'' of philosophers, critics, professors. Are we providing a critical theory of society, a critical reading through texts and film? What is the relationship between a critique and a tactic? Do we stay within the university? If not, how can our philosophy or criticism change the world? And art? Do we, like Sartre, ''take our pens for swords''? Do we prolong the idea of progress and improvement of the human lot, or do we relativize the ups and downs and shifts of power? And what are our own implications for power? As my analyst used to say: Stop trying to change the world.

A difference between France and America may have to do with the position of the intellectual (I retain the word for the sake of convenience). In France, people are bureaucrats, *fonctionnaires d'état*, integrated on a fixed pay scale, as well as writers, artists, philosophers. In the United States, we are first and foremost professors—teachers for the rest of the world, like the customs official stamping my passport each time upon return—and nonexistent without an academic affiliation. Our departments function on a managerial model of effectiveness, growth, and gain, unlike that in which I taught at Vincennes-Saint Denis, where the secretary, her dog, the faculty, and students all shared the same room and semiautomatic typewriter. American universities are leaning more and more toward the corporate world, to the point of losing their nonprofit status—as we read in the *Chronicle of Higher Education* in June 1988. Free agency has also hit the academic market. We are negotiating ourselves as theoreticians preaching dispossession. Presses sell ideas. A recent article in the *Minneapolis Star Tribune* showed how the University of Minnesota Press attracts buyers through alluring covers. And their bestsellers today are Terry Eagleton's *Literary Theory* and Lyotard's *Postmodern Condition*. Marxism sells and so does feminism. The main buyers of French ideas, from existentialism to the new novel and recent theories, have been the Americans. The book that is intended to shape our lives, as readers and as writers, is also an object of commodity, a geometrical shape, a cultural good to be marketed. Ironically, in our era of market conglomerates, what is coveted most is information. Information is the spice of Frank Herbert's *Dune*. And a company like Murdoch and Triangle, which just concluded a multibillion-dollar deal with the acquisition of the most widely read publication in the United States, *TV Guide*, also owns the *New York Post*, the *Financial Times* of London, *Seventeen*, and the *Village Voice*. There is no way that we can *not* be a part of the market world against which we speak. In an interview about the transaction, one CEO coined a new term for the postmodern era, a condensation of information and entertainment into *infotainment*. Infotainment rationally exploits collective irrationality. It erodes text in favor of more pervasive images linked to the cryptic message—a style that reigns in *USA Today*, which one can buy in Paris as well as at the entrance points to the North Woods. But intellectuals cannot ignore massification, a twentieth-century phenomenon they too often simply refer to as "the marketplace." They are part of the world they criticize, and use to some degree its mottos of "bigger and better." Critical theories easily become institutionalized, and too quickly become currency in academic bargaining and lose their cutting edge, their *coup du tranchant*.

Filmmakers for whom the economic contradiction is a matter of life and death have been more frank. As Wim Wenders has shown in *The American Friend* and other films, there is a tension between the artisan filmmaker and big production. Wenders somewhat unilaterally makes the division between American money and European artistry. But we too are caught in the ideology of this dilemma— and how do we resolve it? Pay scales easily show where society's values are situated. The difference in salaries between a football player or a movie star and a professor is that of a couple of zeros. Yet the player and the star are also pawns in a larger system and the game and movie disappear in favor of sheer profit. The existential heroism of a football game of thirty years ago has given way to a two-dimensional game, a flattened image subjugated to a network of concessions, "food enterprises," advertisements that market research strategically controls for maximum gain. In this sense, America has in its way truly become a *communauté désoeuvrée*.

This is well known in the art market, where artists and gallery owners like Julian Schnabel and Mary Boone, in collusion, are making money. Paintings are auctioned off and put in a closet by insurance companies that purchase them for tax write-offs. In more than one sense, the artwork disappears. And this pertains not just to mass goods and imposters but to worthy avant-garde artists as well, artists like Jasper Johns and Claes Oldenburg, whose work was once thought to be subversive. Oldenburg recently took part, with three thousand artists present, in what the *Minneapolis Star Tribune* called an ''event,'' an unveiling of a sculpture garden at the Walker Art Center in Minneapolis, built at a cost of $12.8 million, with no one but Tom Conley protesting the disappearance of the softball field it replaced. An avant-garde filmmaker like Spike Lee, whose *She's Gotta Have It* was based on Godard's and Truffaut's New Wave technical devices of thirty years ago with a script based on recently gathered statistics, is offered a big contract by Columbia Pictures the second time around and is making TV ads for Nike shoes. It is his financial success that opened possibilities for other black filmmakers. Gone is the ideal of the nineteenth-century *artiste maudit*. Artists are center stage, right up there with big businessmen and college administrators. Grants made available by owners of grocery and department stores, or by former lumber barons, are plentiful.

I am essaying a sociological presentation of what Lyotard and others have theorized in their works. All this to note that money is increasingly the determining factor that makes and breaks communities. Many of the young around '68 dropped out to lead alternative lives, often in communes. The dream of today seems to be to get rich quickly, to fall victim to drugs, to rehabilitate, to tell a compelling tale about the process, then to make a movie or play the stock market and retire. Some academics may still speak, somewhat naively, of high art and low art, and deplore the snobbery of the former over the latter when in fact it is all reversed. It is the money commanded by the low arts that imposes. It cost more a couple of weeks ago to see Prince perform than it did to hear Leontyne Price.

What then does it mean for intellectuals in this context: to contest, to act? Who is performing self-criticism? We do not believe in model societies or model communities, and we know that neither the proletariat nor women will lead us to the promised land. Any change in power brings with it another configuration of power. On the one hand, it is difficult not to agree with Lyotard in his dialogic meditation on revolutionary discourse:

> In historical-political reality, it is necessary to ''let this subject speak.''—
> Aren't its phrases the signs in question (No. 236): suffering, class anger and hatred, enthusiasm and solidarity? And only these signs?—But if these signs have a universal value, they are on the side of the audience (Kant Notice 4:§5), they have an aesthetic and not a ''practical'' value.''[5]

On the other hand, no one seems to follow the simple, if somewhat romantic, precept of Gilles Deleuze, quoting Faulkner, in *Mille Plateaux*: One has to *become* black in order not to be fascist (emphasis mine). We have seen the Vietcong turn against their neighbors, the Israelis against the Arabs. Certain events are privileged, while others go unnoticed. The Jewish question in France is much debated and Auschwitz has become the unavowable event. Little is being said about continuous "events," like that through which American Indians—of whom there were perhaps twenty million when Europeans first arrived—have been decimated to just over a million. We militate for the abolition of apartheid and the release of Nelson Mandela, its literary representative. But next to the picture in the paper giving our protest coverage, there is another article in small type about 75,000 families in the Mississippi Valley living on an annual income of less than $5,000 per family. And a few pages later, a triumphant Donald Trump shows off his yacht bought for $30 million from the Arabs, presumably to help the balance of payments: "I look at this ship as one of the great jewels of the world, and as an American, I'm proud to have pulled it back here. I think Americans should have the jewels, should go out and buy the jewels of the world because we're a great country."[6]

Derrida's critique of metaphysics and Foucault's historical genealogy may have had certain claims to universal intentions. The *relance du concept*, a remarking of the concept, was to take us out of oppositional categories, while Foucault's analysis of power was to expose the mastery of the subject through power that underlies the models of the human sciences. They both wanted to get out of a constituted self. Foucault even somewhat flatly declared the end of man. Lyotard's project is twofold: to defend and illustrate philosophy against the *genre économique* and against university authority. The problem at work in translating Lyotard into our conditions is that the American university is a corporate university and we are a part of it. Through the blatant marketing of our theories we are back in capitalism. At the same time, we cannot not market our theories. Lyotard, setting aside his all-pervasive notion of desire from earlier texts, following Wittgenstein, Frege, Kripke, figures that it is economically productive to show that existence does not exist. "The ontological argument is false. Nothing can be said about reality that does not presuppose it."[7] And elsewhere: "The picture's form, its propositional form when the picture is a logical one, constitutes a kind of standard measurement (*Masstab*) which comes to be laid against (*angelegt*) reality. . . . It can do this only if reality is shaped the same way as the picture. But how can this conformity or communality [*communauté*] be proved?"[8] The ultimate in unmooring, it may, of course, also be the ultimate in power and lead to a new one-upmanship where nothing can ever be decided.

Habermas, following Frege and Kripke himself—with vigor and keen ruse, no less—decides in favor of a tactic: a temporary consensus among people who, though their speeches are made of different forces, would decide on one. Ignoring much of the work done in *The Differend*, presumably basing his criticism on earlier works by Lyotard on Freud and Nietzsche, Habermas decries the postmodern position of the observer. For Habermas, we're all in it, part of a community that is decided temporarily by a course of action. What is convincing about his strategy, his call to communicative action based on consent and his nonparanoid relation to the world, is undermined by the blindness of his accusation. Freud and Nietzsche both had shown that the observer is already the observed, is already in a position of countertransference. The way we choose, consciously and unconsciously, to approach the world—as technocrats, revolutionaries, and brokers, or as philosophers and professors of literature—has much to do with our perspective on the world. It is our *libidinal economy*, to use an earlier term of Lyotard's, that prompts our ways of investigating and reading the world, along with socialization and a historical positioning.

However, what is my position from the university, dealing as I do with feminism, literature, and film? With money as the real force pervading our very gestures of self-criticism, action, contestation, and the like? With the dominance of the economic genre to which all other genres, including the political, are subjected, the field of action may likely be in politics or the legal professions. It is really through legal measures that issues get decided. But ideas raise consciousness.

To come back to my earlier question of linking: what about feminism as an emancipatory discourse when it is, perhaps, no longer even a question of giving a language to the oppressed? New issues are emerging, such as ecology and the plight of the homeless, estimated at several million in the United States. The issues crosscut gender, class, and race. French feminists have only indirectly dealt with linking their discourses to the economic genre: Kristeva turns to psychoanalysis to praise the "solitary, playful modern subject" (*In the Beginning Was Love: Psychoanalysis and Faith*); Irigaray analyzes sexuality through linguistics ("Le Sexe linguistique," in *Languages* 85, 21 [March 1987]); Wittig's fighting women of *Virgile-non* seem more tuned into memories of '68. And Cixous's mystical and lyrical writings, shifting from the scene of the unconscious to the scene of history through *Manne* or her plays, avoid the problem by rejecting it.

Most feminist discourses of French stamp have followed major currents, criticizing a philosophy of the subject along the division of body/mind, reason and unreason. Woman has been given somewhat mystifying attributes: darkness, night, enigmatic, fascinating, nonexistent, inaccessible, and the like. Temporary, strategic insistence on going back to various pre-stages of language may have been necessary but these are becoming increasingly difficult to link to sexuality in an age of mass production. Ultimately, it is not the state that oppresses the subject through rationalization, but the economic genre that exploits the masses by appealing precisely to their unreason and emotions. Hysteria is no longer a disease of the lonely madwoman but is mass produced for economic exploitation. "Infotainment" does away with any rationality at all costs, for the sake of saving money.

French feminists—though themselves hardly ever on the side of undeci-dability—have dealt primarily with questions of the origin and Freudian models of repression, with whether the maternal body speaks or whether it is silent—an orthodox position still defended by some, like Kristeva. They fought (male) so-cialization as repressing instinctual forces, as making a division between cultural and noncultural—the barbaric, closer to the body, a romantic paradigm often re-layed via Nietzsche. They wrote in the wake of crossing the boundaries between theory and fiction. This is not to downplay their personal differences through an easy synthesis. Nor especially to mitigate the impact of those theories, with their insistence on the scene of the unconscious and a viewing of the other as other (self) rather than as nonself, with a negative inflection. Their very strength may have been in their insistence on being perpetually in dialogue, in quest, on re-ducing to a minimum the conceptual moment of repression. Their concern is with how the word, in dialogue, links, touches the addressee. A form of practical the-orizing allows them—and this is politically vital—to bridge the gap between the-ory and its empirical practice, a gap often to be deplored. Their community is never homogeneous but put together by heterogeneous elements in solidarity. French feminist theories have put their emphases on the private sphere, on deliv-erance and pleasure. They do away with the necessity of linking with a world of public (masculine) glory and so run the risk, perhaps, of failing to link up with various other discourses in the world.

Their aesthetics, from those of the new novel, from generators and linguistic patterns, have evolved, in contact with Bataille and Nietzsche, to ecstasy and ravishment, to a refinement in communication with the other so extreme that it reaches the point of becoming ethereal. From writing a world to come, they have come full circle in the face of the economic genre to nostalgically regretting a past world without technology, a community that never was. Yet to be effective, the link with that world must be made. Massification can be neither sneered at nor ignored.

What struck me a year ago was what I perceived as a gap between feminist theories and the present-day world. It sounded, all of a sudden, as if those the-ories were written from a sheltered drawing room.

It is to be hoped that these theories with their refined communicational skills might have an impact on practical everyday living, where they would come to touch upon questions of ecology and peace if followed through—and be other than economic currency in an academic power game. How these theories, gen-erally opting for ethical consideration of the living, can be implemented in a country whose economic genre urges for ''hostile takeovers'' remains to be seen. The United States, where women are the most sexually emancipated, curiously favors the reign of the father around whom sons and daughters gravitate. A per-sonality, though in the singular, is already an institution.

Habermas's contribution may have been to urge us to view a certain norma-tivization as a given. His critique of Foucault's theory of power seems of interest for feminist purposes. The body has not become increasingly tyrannized but, rather, some legalization has provided help. *Technobody*, as it has become fash-ionable to say, is not just a crushing word, and our body is certainly not the same as a hundred years ago. Feminism, having explored the body/mind duality, can leave it behind. The days of the hysteric are over and probably those of lengthy sessions on the couch as well.

Statistics show that the sexual revolution and its pleasures have brought about some unpleasures. A staggering percentage of unwed mothers often only mar-ginally provide for children and end up homeless. This is thought not in terms of a social stigma and a moral law, but in terms of a norm: low income, problem children, welfare, drugs. These children with a diminished future are measured, it is true, in terms of a capitalist mode of success. But is there another? Desub-limation has brought about certain side effects but is here to stay, in spite of ru-mors to the contrary. Of importance, though, is not just *jouissance* or pleasure, but legalization of abortion to alleviate human pressures exercised on the earth and help mothers and children in poverty. Certainly theories cannot explain rape, and contrary to popular fiction, it is often the white middle-class man who rapes the white woman, in collusion with his mother. Necessity of normativization is too neglected by French feminists who, living an aesthetic myth of negativity, permanent revolution, or of joyful exposure to the other, are unaware of the im-pact of massification on the way we live.

All depends, as Lyotard reminds us, on where one speaks from, and ours is but a world of differends. The relatively privileged position of the United States on the globe—seldom subjected to natural cataclysms, sheltered largely from ur-gent poverty, and with war kept at a distance—allows us to engage in the activ-ities of our choice, be it as artist, critic, philosopher, lawyer, or politician. All is happening so fast that our positions have to be constantly reevaluated. To repeat: it may be necessary to reevaluate our theories in view of the economic genre of which we are also a part, to attune French feminist writers, with their keen skills in communication, to our everyday world. It may be economically productive to leave aside undecidability, something that most feminists have always done—and establish more direct links with the present-day world.

I have gone at full speed and high altitude, without giving you the advantage of following your journey on a little videodisc, the electronic device replacing the narrative voice of the invisible pilot, and my remarks turned out to be general and only marginally communal. In movement, my aerial view is far from that of Montesquieu in his tower. This is how I read the world following the remarks made by Jean-François Lyotard last year. Again, it all depends on where one chooses to speak from. And as a critic of literature and film, I am less intent on

drawing up a social theory of the world than I am on reading critically, in dialogue with artistic practices of all kinds, to see and listen to how they might bring about different ways of reading the world for others and for ourselves. As the French like to say: My words do not seek to apply a theory, nor are they ignorant of all of theory.

The exclusive building of bigger and better elephants — as in the joke — leaves people with a void. Hence perhaps the popularity of New Age, that form of mysticism, formalized by the passage of Godfrey Reggio and Phillip Glass's *Koyaanisqatsi*, life out of balance, to *Powaqqatsi*, life in transformation. It may be an illusory dream, but we have to gamble and be vigilant at all times, to theorize and practice, to criticize not just a system but ourselves, to replace the great moral law with the law of the living, as Cixous would have it: To live and let live, to do away with a purely quantitative evaluation of the world.

How to navigate between relativism and normativization, to be less obsessed with death, to think of an affirmation of life, to fly but touch the ground, lighting here and there, was suggested at a local theater this summer by the latest film by Wim Wenders. Wenders, parting from his lunar landscapes of *The State of Things* and the plastic world of simulacra in *Tokyo-ga*, has shown us, in his *Himmel über Berlin*, an attempt at moving from death to life, from apocalypse to a reaching out. *Himmel über Berlin* transforms Jean-Luc Godard's ambiguous first or last couple in *First Name: Carmen* to the first couple of a different sort. Not unlike Resnais/Duras with *Hiroshima Mon Amour*, Wenders/Handke ask what it is like

to live and love in Berlin with history past and present. The answer is quite different and the insistence is on the reaching out, on holding out the hand. (The French *maintenant*, now, is not just an appropriation of the hand—*tenir la main*, to hold the hand—as Lyotard said in a recent seminar, but a holding-as-caress, on a passage from death to life.) In the Wenders film, the metaphor of flying is all-pervasive: from wings mechanical to wings human, animal, and celestial; from planes to angels; from the wingless man falling to his death and from bird statues to the double inscription of the bird and flight in the name of Peter Falk, alias Colombo. Mechanical wings, bronze wings, absence of wings, chicken wings: the insistence is on flying and on touching down, not on fleeing.

From my cabin where I write, I look over the Vermilion River where the solitary bald eagle flies, a symbol of nineteenth-century freedom that has found its way in these days of time efficiency onto the envelopes of Express Mail, with which we destine at great cost our amorous or scholarly pronouncements. But I also see the ubiquitous poplars quaking high up in the wind. The tree book tells me their Latin name: *Populus tremuloides*, which I loosely translate as the community of trembling people. A move from the fear and trembling of a paternal Abraham or a solitary Nietzschean subject to that of a trembling people, a trembling community, would perhaps be a way of reading the world.

Did I work myself out of a crisis into a resolution? And ''crisis'' after all is a historical term opening our era of modernity. But perhaps there is no crisis, no resolution and no destiny, only a trembling, an agitation in the wind, and the

7054. TOTAL, außen, tags (9 Sek.)
in dem ein Sonnenstrahl durch die Wolken bricht.
Tief unten am Horizont die Stadt Berlin. Im Himmel erscheint die Schrift

Nous sommes embarqués. (Wir sind eingeschifft.)

question would less be that of a gap than of a continuous linking, unlinking, in movement, and of a (non-)communal: *qu'est-ce qui nous agite?*

Notes

1. Jean-François Lyotard, *The Differend: Phrases in Dispute,* trans. Georges Van Den Abbeele (Minneapolis: University of Minnesota Press, 1988), 181.

2. Jürgen Habermas, *Der philosophische Diskurs der Moderne: 12 Vorlesungen* (Frankfurt: Suhrkampf Verlag, 1985); translated into French by Christian Bouchindhomme and Rainer Rochlitz, *Le Discours philosophique de la modernité* (Paris: Gallimard, Coll. "Bibliothèque de Philosophie," 1988); David B. Downing, "Deconstruction's Scruples: The Politics of Enlightened Critique," *Diacritics* 17, 3 (Fall 1987), 66–81.

3. Jürgen Habermas, *The Theory of Communicative Action,* vol. 1, *Reason and the Rationalization of Society,* trans. Thomas McCarthy (Boston: Beacon Press, 1984), xxxv. Quoted by Downing in "Deconstruction's Scruples," 73.

4. Hélène Cixous, "La Crise dans la littérature," *Les Lettres françaises* 221 (Nov. 25–30, 1970); see also Verena Andermatt Conley, "Epilogue," in *Lire Les Lettres françaises: périmètres et limites d'une idéologie,* Ph.D. thesis, University of Wisconsin, 1974.

5. Lyotard, *Differend,* 172.

6. *Minneapolis Stor Tribune,* August 18, 1988.

7. Lyotard, *Differend,* 32.

8. Ibid., 38.

Democratic Citizenship and the Political Community

Chantal Mouffe

The themes of "citizenship" and "community" are being discussed in many quarters of the left today. It is no doubt a consequence of the crisis of "class" politics and indicates the growing awareness of the need for a new form of identification around which to organize the forces struggling for the radicalization of democracy. I do indeed agree that the question of political identity is the crucial one, and I consider that to attempt to construct "citizens' " identities should be an important task of democratic politics. But there are many different visions of citizenship and central issues are at stake in their contestation. The way we define citizenship is intimately linked to the kind of society and political community we want.

How should we understand citizenship when our goal is a radical and plural democracy? Such a project requires the creation of a chain of equivalences among democratic struggles and therefore the creation of a common political identity among democratic subjects. For the interpellation "citizens" to be able to fulfill that role, what conditions must it meet?

Those are the problems I will address and I am going to argue that the key question is how to conceive of the nature of the political community under modern democratic conditions. I consider that we need to go beyond the conceptions of citizenship of both the liberal and the civic republican traditions while building upon their respective strengths.

To situate my reflections in the context of the current discussions, I will begin by engaging the debate between Kantian liberals and the so-called communitarians. In this way, I hope to bring to the fore the specificity of my approach both politically and theoretically.

Liberalism versus Civic Republicanism

What is really at stake between John Rawls and his communitarian critics is the issue of citizenship. Two different languages for articulating our identity as citizens are confronting each other. Rawls proposes to represent the citizen of a constitutional democracy in terms of equal rights expressed by his two principles of justice. He affirms that once citizens see themselves as free and equal persons, they should recognize that to pursue their own different conceptions of the good, they need the same primary goods (i.e., the same basic rights, liberties, and opportunities) as well as the same all-purpose means (i.e., income and wealth), and the same social bases of self-respect. This is why they should agree on a political conception of justice that states that "all social primary goods—liberty and opportunity, income and wealth, and the bases of self-respect—are to be distributed equally, unless an unequal distribution of any or all of these goods is to the advantage of the least favored" (Rawls, *A Theory of Justice*, 302–3). According to that liberal view, citizenship is the capacity for each person to form, revise, and rationally pursue his/her definition of the good. Citizens are seen as using their rights to promote their self-interest within certain constraints imposed by the exigency to respect the rights of others. The communitarians object that it is an impoverished conception that precludes the notion of the citizen as one for whom it is natural to join with others to pursue common action in view of the common good. Michael Sandel has argued that Rawls's conception of the self is an "unencumbered" one that leaves no room for a "constitutive" community, a community that would constitute the very identity of the individuals. It only allows for an "instrumental" community, a community in which individuals with their previously defined interests and identity enter in view of furthering those interests (*Liberalism and the Limits of Justice*).

For the communitarians, the alternative to this flawed liberal approach is the revival of the civic republican view of politics that puts a strong emphasis on the notion of a public good, prior to and independent of individual desires and interests. Such a tradition has almost disappeared today because it has been displaced by liberalism, though it has a long history. It received its full expression in the Italian republics at the end of the Middle Ages, but its origins go back to Greek and Roman thought. It was reformulated in England in the seventeenth century by James Harrington, John Milton, and other republicans. Later it traveled to the New World through the work of the neo-Harringtonians, and recent studies have shown that it played an important role during the American Revolution.

There are indeed serious problems with the liberal conception of citizenship, but we must be aware of the shortcomings of the civic republican solution, too. It does provide us with a view of citizenship much richer than the liberal one, and its conception of politics as the realm where we can recognize ourselves as participants in a political community has obvious appeal for the critics of liberal individualism. Nevertheless, there is a real danger of coming back to a premodern view of politics that does not acknowledge the novelty of modern democracy and the crucial contribution of liberalism. The defense of pluralism, the idea of individual liberty, the separation of church and state, the development of civil society, all these are constitutive of democratic politics. They require distinguishing between the domain of the private and the domain of the public, the realm of morality and the realm of politics. Contrary to what some communitarians propose, a modern democratic political community cannot be organized around a single substantive idea of the common good. The recovery of a strong participatory idea of citizenship should not be done at the cost of sacrificing individual liberty. This is the point where the communitarian critique of liberalism takes a dangerous conservative turn.

The problem, I believe, is not to replace one tradition with the other but to draw on both and to try to combine their insights in a new conception of citizenship adequate for a project of radical and plural democracy. While liberalism did certainly contribute to the formulation of the idea of a universal citizenship, based on the assertion that all individuals are born free and equal, it also reduced citizenship to a mere legal status, indicating the possession of rights that the individual holds against the state. The way those rights are exercised is irrelevant as long as their holders do not break the law or interfere with the rights of others. Social cooperation aims only at enhancing our productive capacities and facilitating the attainment of each person's individual prosperity. Ideas of public-spiritedness, civic activity, and political participation in a community of equals are alien to most liberal thinkers.

Civic republicanism, on the contrary, emphasizes the value of political participation and attributes a central role to our insertion in a political community. But the problem arises with the exigency of conceiving the political community in a way that is compatible with liberal pluralism. In other words, we are faced with the old dilemma of how to reconcile the liberties of the ancients with the liberties of the moderns. The liberals argue that they are incompatible and that today ideas about the "common good" can only have totalitarian implications. According to them, it is impossible to combine democratic institutions with the sense of common purpose that premodern society enjoyed and the ideals of "republican virtue" are nostalgic relics to be discarded. Active political participation, they say, is incompatible with the modern idea of liberty. Individual liberty can only be understood in a negative way as absence of coercion.

This argument, powerfully restated by Isaiah Berlin in "Two Concepts of Liberty," is generally used to discredit any attempt to recapture the civic republican conception of politics. However, it has recently been challenged by Quentin Skinner, who argues that there is no basic or necessary incompatibility between the classical republican conception of citizenship and modern democracy. He finds in several forms of republican thought, particularly in Machiavelli, a way of conceiving liberty that though negative—and therefore modern—includes, however, political participation and civic virtue. It is negative because liberty is conceived as the absence of impediments to the realization of our chosen ends. But it also asserts that it is only as citizens of a "free state," of a community whose members participate actively in the government, that such individual liberty can be guaranteed. To ensure our own liberty and avoid the servitude that would render its exercise impossible, we must cultivate civic virtues and devote ourselves to the common good. The idea of a common good above our private interest is a necessary condition for enjoying individual liberty. Skinner's argument is important because it refutes the liberals' claim that individual liberty and political participation can never be reconciled. This is crucial for a radical democratic project, but the kind of political community adequate for such an articulation between the rights of the individual and the political participation of the citizen then becomes the question to be envisaged.

Modern Democracy and Political Community

Another way to approach the debate between Kantian liberals like Rawls and the communitarians is through the question of the priority of the right over the good, which has a direct relevance for the issue of the modern democratic political community.

For Rawls, such a priority indicates that individual rights cannot be sacrificed for the sake of the general welfare, as is the case with utilitarianism, and that the principles of justice impose restrictions on what are the permissible conceptions of the good that individuals are allowed to pursue. This is why he insists that the principles of justice must be derived independently of any particular conception of the good, since they need to respect the existence of a plurality of competing conceptions of the good in order to be accepted by all citizens. His aim here is to defend liberal pluralism, which requires not imposing upon men any specific conception of well-being or particular plan of life. Those are for liberals private questions bearing on individual morality, and they believe that each person should be able to organize his or her life according to his or her own wishes, without unnecessary interferences. Hence the centrality of the concept of individual rights and the assertion that principles of justice must not privilege a particular conception of the good life.

I consider this an important principle that needs defending because it is crucial for modern democratic societies. Indeed, modern democracy is precisely characterized by the absence of a substantive common good. This is the meaning of the democratic revolution as analyzed by Claude Lefort, who identifies it with the dissolution of landmarks of certainty. According to Lefort, modern democratic society is a society where power has become an empty space and is separated from law and knowledge (*Political Forms*, 305ff.). In such a society, there is no more possibility of providing a final guarantee, a definite legitimation, because there is no more power incorporated in the person of the prince and related to a transcendental instance. Power, law, and knowledge are therefore exposed to a radical indeterminacy: in my terms, a substantive common good becomes impossible. This is also what Rawls indicates when he affirms that "we must abandon the hope of a political community if by such a community we mean a political society united in affirming a general and comprehensive doctrine" ("The Idea of an Overlapping Consensus," 10). If the priority of the right over the good were restricted to that, there would not be anything for me to disagree with. But Rawls wants to establish an absolute priority of the right over the good because he does not recognize that it can only exist in a certain type of society with specific institutions and that it is a consequence of the democratic revolution.

To that, the communitarians reply—with reason—that such an absolute priority of the right cannot exist and that it is only through our participation in a community which defines the good in a certain way that we can acquire a sense of the right and a conception of justice. And Charles Taylor correctly points out that the mistake with the liberal approach is that "it fails to take account of the degree to which the free individual with his own goals and aspirations whose just rewards it is trying to protect, is himself only possible within a certain kind of civilization; that it took a long development of certain institutions and practices, of the rule of law, of rules of equal respect, of habits of common deliberation, of common association, of cultural development and so on, to produce the modern individual" (*Philosophy and the Human Sciences*, 200).

Where the communitarians go astray is when some of them, like Sandel, conclude that there can never be a priority of the right over the good and that we should therefore reject liberal pluralism and go back to a type of community organized around shared moral values and a substantive idea of the common good. We can perfectly agree with Rawls about the priority of justice as the principal virtue of social and political institutions and in defending pluralism and rights, while admitting that those principles are specific to a certain type of political association. There is, however, another aspect of the communitarian critique of liberalism that we should not abandon but reformulate. The absence of a single substantive common good in modern democratic societies and the separation between the realm of morality and the realm of politics have, no doubt, signified an incontestable gain in individual freedom. But the consequences for politics have been damaging. All normative concerns have increasingly been relegated to the field of private morality, to the domain of "values," and politics has been stripped of its ethical components. An instrumentalist conception has become dominant, concerned exclusively with the compromise between already defined interests. On the other hand, liberalism's exclusive concern with individuals and their rights has not provided content and guidance for the exercise of those rights. This has led to the devaluation of civic activity, of a common concern, which has caused an increasing lack of social cohesion in democratic societies. The communitarians are right to criticize such a situation, and I agree with their attempt to revive some aspects of the classical conception of politics. We need indeed to reestablish the lost connection between ethics and politics, but it cannot be done by sacrificing the gains of the democratic revolution. We should not accept a false dichotomy between individual liberty and rights on one side versus civic activity and political community on the other. Our choice is not at all between an aggregate of individuals without common public concern and a premodern community organized around a single substantive idea of the common good. How to envisage the modern democratic political community outside this dichotomy is the crucial question.

I have already pointed out how Quentin Skinner indicates a possible form of articulation between individual freedom and civic participation. But we must also be able to formulate the ethical character of modern citizenship in a way that is compatible with moral pluralism and respects the priority of the right over the good. What we share and what makes us fellow citizens in a liberal democratic regime is not a substantive idea of the good but a set of political principles specific to such a tradition: the principles of freedom and equality for all. Those principles constitute what we can call, following Wittgenstein, a "grammar" of political conduct. To be a citizen is to recognize the authority of those principles and the rules in which they are embodied—to have them informing our political judgment and our actions. To be associated in terms of the recognition of the liberal democratic principles, this is the meaning of citizenship that I want to put forward. It implies seeing citizenship not as a legal status but as a form of identification, a type of political identity: something to be constructed, not empirically given. Since there will always be competing interpretations of the democratic principles of equality and liberty there will therefore be competing interpretations of democratic citizenship. I will inquire into the nature of a radical democratic citizenship, but before going to that point I must further tackle the question of the political association or community.

The Political Community: Universitas or Societas?

As I indicated previously, we need to conceive of a mode of political association that, although it does not postulate the existence of a substantive common good, nevertheless implies the idea of commonality, of an ethico-political bond that creates a linkage among the participants in the association, allowing us to speak of a political "community" even if it is not in the strong sense. In other words, what we are looking for is a way to accommodate the distinctions between public and private, morality and politics, which have been the great contribution of liberalism to modern democracy, without renouncing the ethical nature of the political association.

I consider that, if we interpret them in a certain way, the reflections on civil association proposed by Michael Oakeshott in *On Human Conduct* can be very illuminating for such a purpose. Oakeshott shows that *societas* and *universitas*, which were understood in the late Middle Ages as two different modes of human association, can also represent alternative interpretations of the modern state. *Universitas* indicates an engagement in an enterprise to pursue a common substantive purpose or to promote a common interest. It refers, therefore, to "persons associated in a manner such as to constitute them a natural person, a partnership of persons which is itself a Person, or in some important respects like a person" (203).

Contrary to that model of association of agents engaged in a common enterprise defined by a purpose, *societas* or "civil association" designates a formal relationship in terms of rules, not a substantive relation in terms of common action. "The idea *societas* is that of agents who, by choice or circumstance, are related to one another so as to compose an identifiable association of a certain sort. The tie which joins them, and in respect of which each recognizes himself to be *socius*, is not that of an engagement in an enterprise to pursue a common substantive purpose or to promote a common interest, but that of loyalty to one another" (201). It is not a mode of relation, therefore, in terms of common action but a relation in which participants are related to one another in the acknowledgment of the authority of certain conditions in acting.

Oakeshott insists that the participants in a *societas* or *cives* are not associated for a common enterprise nor in a view of facilitating the attainment of each person's individual prosperity; what links them is the recognition of the authority of the conditions specifying their common or "public" concern, a "practice of civility." This public concern or consideration of *cives*, Oakeshott calls *respublica*. It is a practice of civility that consists in a manifold of rules or rulelike prescriptions that do not prescribe performances, satisfactions to be sought, or actions to be performed but "moral considerations specifying conditions to be subscribed to in choosing performances" (182).

It seems to me that Oakeshott's idea of the civil association as *societas* is adequate to define political association under modern democratic conditions. Indeed, it is a mode of human association that recognizes the disappearance of a single substantive idea of the common good and makes room for individual liberty. It is a form of association that can be enjoyed among relative strangers belonging to many purposive associations and whose allegiances to specific communities are not seen as conflicting with their membership in the civil association. This would not be possible if such an association were conceived as *universitas*, as purposive association, because it would not allow for the existence of other genuine purposive associations in which individuals would be free to participate.

To belong to the political community, what is required is to accept a specific language of civil intercourse, the *respublica*. Those rules prescribe norms of conduct to be subscribed to in seeking self-chosen satisfactions and in performing self-chosen actions. The identification with those rules of civil intercourse creates a common political identity among persons otherwise engaged in many different enterprises. This modern form of political community is held together not by a substantive idea of a common good but by a common bond, a public concern. It is therefore a community without a definite shape, a definite identity, and in continuous reenactment.

Such a conception is clearly different from the premodern idea of the political community, but it is also different from the liberal idea of political association. For liberalism also sees political association as a form of purposive association, of enterprise, except that in its case the aim is an instrumental one: the promotion of self-interest.

Oakeshott criticizes the liberal view of the state as a conciliator of interests, which he considers to be as remote from civil association as the idea of the state as promoter of an interest, and he declares, ''It has been thought that 'the Rule of Law' is enough to identify civil association, whereas what is significant is the kind of law: 'moral' or 'instrumental' '' (318). Oakeshott's conception should therefore not be confounded with the liberal doctrine of the rule of law. He stresses the moral character of the *respublica* and affirms that political thought concerns the *respublica* in terms of *bonum civile*. He declares: ''Civility, then, denotes an order of moral (not instrumental) considerations, and the so-called neutrality of civil prescriptions is a half truth which needs to be supplemented by the recognition of civil association as itself a moral and not a prudential condition'' (175). By ''moral'' Oakeshott obviously refers not to a comprehensive view but to what I have proposed to call the ''ethico-political'' since he asserts that what is civilly desirable cannot be inferred or derived from general moral principles and that political deliberation is concerned with moral considerations of its own: ''This *respublica* is the articulation of a common concern that the pursuit of all purposes and the promotion of all interests, the satisfaction of all wants and the propagation of all beliefs shall be in subscription to conditions formulated in rules indifferent to the merits of any interest or the truth or error of any belief and consequently not itself a substantive interest or doctrine'' (172).

We could say, using Rawls's vocabulary, that in a civil association or *societas* there exists a priority of the right over the good, but in Oakeshott's case, the principles that specify the right, the *respublica*, are conceived not in a Kantian manner as in Rawls, but in a Hegelian way, since for him, to be associated in terms of the recognition of the *respublica* is to enjoy a "sittlich" relation. What I find useful in this approach is that, while allowing for the recognition of pluralism and individual liberty, the notion of *societas* does not relinquish all normative aspects to the sphere of private morality. This mode of association that Oakeshott traces to Machiavelli, Montesquieu, and Hegel permits us to maintain a certain idea of the political community in the sense of a noninstrumental, an ethical, type of bond among *cives*, while severing it from the existence of a substantive common good.

I did mention at the outset that to be useful for a radical democratic project Oakeshott's reflections needed to be interpreted in a certain way. I am, of course, perfectly aware of the conservative use he makes of the distinction between *societas* and *universitas*, but I believe that it is not the only and necessary one. To be sure, Oakeshott's conservatism resides in the content he puts in the *respublica*, and that can obviously be remedied without problems by putting in it more radical principles, as I will indicate later. But more fundamentally, his conservatism lies in his flawed idea of politics. For his conception of politics as a shared language of civility is only adequate for one aspect of politics: the point of view of the "we," the friend's side. However, as Carl Schmitt rightly pointed out, the criterion of the political is the friend/enemy relation. What is completely missing in Oakeshott is division and antagonism—that is, the aspect of the "enemy." It is an absence that must be remedied if we want to appropriate his notion of *societas*.

To introduce conflict and antagonism into Oakeshott's model, it is necessary to recognize that the *respublica* is the product of a given hegemony, the expression of power relations, and that it can be challenged. Politics is to a great extent about the rules of the *respublica* and their many possible interpretations; it is about the constitution of the political community, not something that takes place inside the political community, as some communitarians would have it. Political life concerns collective, public action; it aims at the construction of a "we" in a context of diversity and conflict. But to construct a "we," it must be distinguished from the "they" and that means establishing a frontier, defining an "enemy." Therefore, while politics aims at constructing a political community and creating a unity, a fully inclusive political community and a final unity can never be realized since there will permanently be a "constitutive outside," an exterior to the community that makes its existence possible. Antagonistic forces will never disappear, and politics is characterized by conflict and division. Forms of agreement can be reached, but they are always partial and provisional since consensus is by necessity based upon acts of exclusion. We are indeed very far from the language of civility dear to Oakeshott!

A Radical Democratic Citizenship

What becomes of the idea of citizenship in such a perspective? If we understand citizenship as the political identity that is created through identification with the *respublica*, a new conception of the citizen becomes possible. First, we are now dealing with a type of political identity, a form of identification, and no longer simply with a legal status. The citizen is not, as in liberalism, someone who is the passive recipient of specific rights and who enjoys the protection of the law. It is not that those elements become irrelevant, but the definition of the citizen shifts because the emphasis is put on the identification with the *respublica*. It is a common political identity of persons who might be engaged in many different purposive enterprises and with differing conceptions of the good, but who accept submission to the rules prescribed by the *respublica* in seeking their satisfactions and in performing their actions. What binds them together is their common recognition of a set of ethico-political values. In this case, citizenship is not just one identity among others—as in liberalism—or the dominant identity that overrides all others—as in civic republicanism. It is an articulating principle that affects the different subject positions of the social agent (as I will show when I discuss the distinction public/private) while allowing for a plurality of specific allegiances and for the respect of individual liberty.

Since we are dealing with politics, however, there will be competing forms of identification linked to different interpretations of the *respublica*. In a liberal democratic regime, we can conceive of the *respublica* as constituted by the political principles of such a regime: equality and liberty for all. If we put such a content into Oakeshott's notion of *respublica* we can affirm that the conditions to be subscribed to and taken into account in acting are to be understood as the exigency of treating the others as free and equal persons. This is clearly open to potentially very radical interpretations. For instance, a radical democratic interpretation will emphasize the numerous social relations where relations of domination exist and must be challenged if the principles of liberty and equality are to apply. It should lead to a common recognition among different groups struggling for an extension and radicalization of democracy that they have a common concern and that in choosing their actions they should subscribe to certain rules of conduct; in other words, it should construct a common political identity as radical democratic citizens.

The creation of political identities as radical democratic citizens depends, therefore, on a collective form of identification among the democratic demands found in a variety of movements: women, workers, black, gay, ecological, as well as in several other "new social movements." This is a conception of citizenship that through a common identification with a radical democratic interpretation of the principles of liberty and equality aims at constructing a "we," a chain of equivalence among their demands so as to articulate them through the principle of democratic equivalence. For it is a matter not of establishing a mere alliance between given interests but of actually modifying the very identity of these forces. This is something many pluralist liberals do not understand because they are blind to relations of power. They agree on the need to extend the sphere of rights in order to include groups hitherto excluded, but they see that process as a smooth one of progressive inclusion into citizenship. This is the typical story as told by T. H. Marshall in his celebrated article "Citizenship and Social Class." The problem with such an approach is that it ignores the limits imposed on the extension of pluralism by the fact that some existing rights have been constituted on the very exclusion or subordination of the rights of other categories. Those identities must first be deconstructed if several new rights are to be recognized.

To make possible a hegemony of the democratic forces, new identities are therefore required and I am arguing here in favor of a common political identity as radical democratic citizens. By that I understand a collective identification with a radical democratic interpretation of the principles of the liberal-democratic regime: liberty and equality. Such an interpretation presupposes that those principles are understood in a way that takes account of the different social relations and subject positions in which they are relevant: gender, class, race, ethnicity, sexual orientation, and so on.

Such an approach can only be adequately formulated within a problematic that conceives of the social agent not as a unitary subject but as the articulation of an ensemble of subject positions, constructed within specific discourses and always precariously and temporarily sutured at the intersection of those subject positions. Only with a non-essentialist conception of the subject which incorporates the psychoanalytic insight that all identities are forms of identification can we pose the question of political identity in a fruitful way. A non-essentialist perspective is also needed concerning the notions of *respublica*, *societas*, and political community. For it is crucial to see them not as empirical referents but as discursive surfaces. Failure to do so would make the type of politics that is posited here completely incomprehensible.

This is the point where a radical democratic conception of citizenship connects with the current debates about "postmodernity" and the critique of rationalism and universalism. The view of citizenship I am proposing rejects the idea of an abstract universalist definition of the public, opposed to a domain of the private seen as the realm of particularity and difference. It considers that, although the modern idea of the citizen was indeed crucial for the democratic revolution, it constitutes today an obstacle to its extension. As feminist theorists have argued, the public realm of modern citizenship has been constructed on the very negation of women's participation. This exclusion was seen as indispensable to postulate the generality and universality of the public sphere. The distinction public/private, central as it was for the assertion of individual liberty, also led to identifying the private with the domestic and played an important role in the subordination of women.

To the idea that the exercise of citizenship consists in adopting a universal point of view, made equivalent to Reason and reserved for men, I am opposing the idea that it consists in identifying with the ethico-political principles of modern democracy and that there can be as many forms of citizenship as there are interpretations of those principles.

In this view, the public/private is not abandoned but reformulated. Here again, Oakeshott can help us to find an alternative to the limitations of liberalism. *Societas* is, according to him, a civil condition in which every enterprise is "private" while never immune from the "public" conditions specified in *respublica*. In a *societas*, "every situation is an encounter between 'private' and 'public,' between an action or an utterance to procure an imagined and wished-for substantive satisfaction and the conditions of civility to be subscribed to in performing it; and no situation is the one to the exclusion of the other" (183). The wants, choices, and decisions are private because they are the responsibility of each individual, but the performances are public because they are required to subscribe to the conditions specified in the *respublica*. Since the rules of the *respublica* do not enjoin, prohibit, or warrant substantive actions or utterances, and do not tell agents what to do, this mode of association respects individual liberty. But the individual's belonging to the political community and identification with its ethico-political principles are manifested by his or her acceptance of the common concern expressed in the *respublica*. It provides the "grammar" of the citizen's conduct.

In the case of a radical democratic citizen, such an approach allows us to envision how a concern with equality and liberty should inform one's actions in all areas of social life. No sphere is immune from those concerns, and relations of domination can be challenged everywhere. Nevertheless, we are not dealing with a purposive kind of community affirming one single goal for all its members, and the freedom of the individual is preserved.

The distinction between private (individual liberty) and public (*respublica*) is maintained as well as the distinction individual/citizen, but they do not correspond to discrete separate spheres. We cannot say: here end my duties as a citizen and begin my freedoms as an individual. Those two identities exist in a permanent tension that can never be reconciled. But this is precisely the tension between liberty and equality that characterizes modern democracy. It is the very life of such a regime, and any attempt to bring about a perfect harmony, to realize a "true" democracy, can only lead to its destruction. This is why a project of radical and plural democracy recognizes the impossibility of the complete realization of democracy and the final achievement of the political community. Its aim is to use the symbolic resources of the liberal democratic tradition to struggle for the deepening of the democratic revolution, knowing that it is a never-ending process. My thesis here has been that the ideal of citizenship could greatly contribute to such an extension of the principles of liberty and equality. By combining the ideal of rights and pluralism with the ideas of public-spiritedness and ethico-political concern, a new modern democratic conception of citizenship could restore dignity to the political and provide the vehicle for the construction of a radical democratic hegemony.

Community and Its Paradoxes: Richard Rorty's "Liberal Utopia"

Ernesto Laclau

Antifoundationalism has so far produced a variety of intellectual and cultural effects, but few of them have referred to the terrain of politics. It is one of the merits of Richard Rorty's work to have attempted, vigorously and persuasively, to establish such a connection. In his most recent book, *Contingency, Irony, and Solidarity*, he has presented an excellent picture of the intellectual transformation of the West during the last two centuries and, on the basis of it, has drawn the main lines of a social and political arrangement that he has called a "liberal utopia." It is not that Rorty tries to present his (post-)philosophical approach as a theoretical grounding for his political proposal—an attempt (which Rorty rejects) that would simply "reoccupy" with an antifoundationalist discourse the terrain of the lost foundation. It is rather that antifoundationalism, together with a plurality of other narratives and cultural interventions, has created the intellectual climate in which certain social and political arrangements are thinkable.

In this essay I will try to show that, although I certainly agree with most of Rorty's philosophical arguments and positions, his notion of "liberal utopia" presents a series of shortcomings that can be superseded only if the liberal features of Rorty's utopia are reinscribed in the wider framework of what Chantal Mouffe and I have called "radical democracy" (Laclau and Mouffe, *Hegemony and the Socialist Strategy*).

I

Let me summarize, in the first place, the main points of Rorty's argument. At the beginning of the book he asserts his primary thesis in the following terms:

> This book tries to show how things look if we drop the demand for a theory which unifies the public and private, and are content to treat the demands of self-creation and of human solidarity as equally valid, yet forever incommensurable. It sketches a figure whom I call the "liberal ironist." I borrow my definition of "liberal" from Judith Shklar, who says that liberals are the people who think that cruelty is the worst thing we do. I use "ironist" to name the sort of person who faces up to the contingency of his or her own most central beliefs and desires — someone sufficiently historicist and nominalist to have abandoned the idea that those central beliefs and desires refer back to something beyond the reach of time and chance. Liberal ironists are people who include among these ungroundable desires their own hope that suffering will be diminished, that the humiliation of human beings by other human beings may cease. (*Contingency*, xv)

The milieu in which these objectives are attainable is that of a postmetaphysical culture.

The specifically political argument about the contingency of the community is preceded by two chapters on "the contingency of language" and "the contingency of selfhood," which constitute its background. Rorty points out that two hundred years ago two main changes took place in the intellectual life of Europe: the increasing realization that truth is fabricated rather than found — which made possible the utopian politics of reshaping social relations — and the romantic revolution, which led to a vision of art as self-creation rather than as imitation of reality. These changes joined forces and progressively acquired cultural hegemony. German idealism was a first attempt at drawing the intellectual consequences of this transformation, but ultimately failed as a result of confusing the idea that nothing has an internal nature to be represented with the very different one that the spatiotemporal world is a product of the human mind. What actually lies behind these dim intuitions of the romantic period is the increasing realization that there is no intrinsic nature of the real, but that the real will look different depending on the languages with which it is described, and that there is not a metalanguage or neutral language which will allow us to decide between competing first-order languages. Philosophical argument does not proceed through an internal deconstruction of a thesis presented in a certain vocabulary but rather through the presentation of a competing vocabulary.

> Interesting philosophy is rarely an examination of the pros and cons of a thesis. Usually it is, implicitly or explicitly, a contest between an

entrenched vocabulary which has become a nuisance and a half-formed new vocabulary which vaguely promises great things. (9)

At this point, Rorty, faithful to his method, simply drops the old conception of language and embarks upon a new operation of redescription through Donald Davidson's philosophy of language, with its rejection of the idea that language constitutes a medium of either representation or expression, and its similarity with the Wittgensteinian conception of alternative vocabularies as alternative tools. Mary Hesse's "metaphoric redescriptions" and Harold Bloom's "strong poet" are also quoted in this connection.

After having shown the contingency of language, Rorty gives selfhood its turn. Here the main heroes are Nietzsche and (especially) Freud. For Nietzsche it is only the poet who fully perceives the contingency of the self.

> The Western tradition thinks of a human life as a triumph just insofar as it breaks out of the world of time, appearance and idiosyncratic opinion into another world—the world of enduring truth. Nietzsche, by contrast, thinks the important boundary to cross is not the one separating time from atemporal truth but rather the one which divides the old from the new. He thinks a human life triumphant just insofar as it escapes inherited descriptions of the contingencies of its existence and finds new descriptions. This is the difference between the will to truth and the will to self-overcoming. It is the difference between thinking of redemption as making contact with something larger and more enduring than oneself and redemption as Nietzsche describes it: "recreating all 'it was' into a 'thus I willed it.' " (29)

But it is Freud who represents the most important step forward in the process of de-divinization of the self. He showed the way in which all the features of our consciousness can be traced back to the contingency of our upbringing.

> He de-universalizes the moral sense, making it as idiosyncratic as the poet's inventions. He thus let us see the moral consciousness as historically conditioned, a product as much of time and chance as of political or aesthetic consciousness. (30)

In spite of their many points in common, Freud is more useful, according to Rorty, than Nietzsche, because the former shows that the conformist bourgeois is dull only on the surface, before the psychoanalytic exploration, while the latter relegates "the vast majority of humanity to the status of dying animals" (35).

Finally we reach the contingency of the community, which should be dealt with in more detail because it concerns the main topic of this essay. Rorty here finds an initial difficulty: he is attached to both liberal democracy and antifoundationalism, but the vocabulary in which the former was initially presented is that of Enlightenment rationalism. The thesis that he tries to defend in the following two chapters is that, although this vocabulary was essential to liberal democracy in its initial stages, today it has become an impediment to its further progress and consolidation. This involves him in an effort to reformulate the democratic ideal in a nonrationalist and nonuniversalist way.

Rorty starts by clearing out of his path the possible charges of relativism and irrationalism. He quotes Schumpeter as saying, "To realize the relative validity of one's convictions and yet stand for them unflinchingly, is what distinguishes a civilized man from a barbarian"; and he includes Isaiah Berlin's comment on this passage: "To demand more than this is perhaps a deep and incurable metaphysical need; but to allow it to determine one's practice is a symptom of an equally deep, and more dangerous, moral and political immaturity" (46). It is these assertions that Michael Sandel is brought into the picture to oppose: "If one's convictions are only relatively valid, why stand for them unflinchingly?" (46). Thus the relativism debate is opened in its classical terms. Rorty steps into this debate by trying to make a nonissue of the problem of relativism. He starts by discarding two notions of absolute validity: that which identifies the absolutely valid with what is valid to everyone and anyone (because in this case there would be no interesting statement that would be absolutely valid); and that which identifies it with those statements that can be justified to all those who are not corrupted (because this presupposes a division of human nature [divine/animal] that is ultimately incompatible with liberalism). The only alternative is, as a consequence, to restrict the opposition between rational and irrational forms of persuasion to the confines of a language game, where it is possible to distinguish reasons for belief from causes for belief that are not rational. This, however, leaves open the question about the rationality of the shifts of vocabularies and, as there is no neutral ground upon which to decide between them, it looks as if all important shifts in paradigms, metaphorics, or vocabularies would have causes but not reasons. But this would imply that all great intellectual movements such as Christianity, Galilean science, or the Enlightenment should be considered to have irrational origins. This is the point at which Rorty concludes that the usefulness of a description in terms of the opposition rational/irrational vanishes. Davidson— whom Rorty quotes at this point—notes that once the notion of rationality has been restricted to internal coherence, if the use of the term is not also restricted we will find ourselves calling "irrational" many things we appreciate (the decision to repress a certain desire, for instance, will appear irrational from the point of view of the desire itself). If Davidson and Hesse are right, metaphors are causes and not reasons for changes in beliefs, but this does not make them "irrational"; it is the very notion of irrationality that has to be questioned. The consequence is that the question of validity is essentially open and conversational. Only a society in which a system of taboos and a rigid delimitation of the order of subjects have been imposed and accepted by everybody will escape the conversational nature of validity, but this is precisely the kind of society that is strictly incompatible with liberalism:

> It is central to the idea of a liberal society that, with respect to words as opposed to deeds, persuasion as opposed to force, anything goes. This openmindedness should not be fostered because, as Scripture teaches, Truth is great and will prevail, nor because, as Milton suggests, Truth will always win in a free and open encounter. It should be fostered for its own sake. *A liberal society is one which is content to call "true" whatever the upshot of such encounters turns out to be.* That is why a liberal society is badly served by an attempt to supply it with "philosophical foundations." For the attempt to supply such foundations presupposes a natural order of topics and arguments which is prior to, and overrides the results of, encounters between old and new vocabularies. (51–52; emphasis in original)

This question of the relationship between foundationalism (rationalism) and liberalism is treated by Rorty through a convincing critique of Horkheimer and Adorno's *Dialectic of Enlightenment*. He accepts their vision that the forces put into movement by the Enlightenment have undermined the Enlightenment's own convictions, but he does not accept their conclusion that, as a result of this, liberalism is at present intellectually and morally bankrupt. According to Rorty, the vocabularies that presided over the initiation of a historical process or intellectual movement are never adapted to them when they reach maturity, and in his view ironic thinking is far more appropriate to a fully fledged liberal society than rationalism.

The poet and the utopian revolutionary, who are central historical actors in Rorty's account, play the role of "protesting in the name of the society itself against those aspects of the society which are unfaithful to its own self-image." And he adds in a crucial passage:

> This substitution (of the protest of alienated people by the revolutionary and the poet) seems to cancel out the difference between the revolutionary and the reformer. But one can define the *ideally* liberal society as one in which the difference is canceled out. A liberal society is one whose ideals can be fulfilled by persuasion rather than force, by reform rather than revolution, by the free and open encounters of present linguistic and other practices with suggestions for new practices. But this is to say that an ideal liberal society is one which has no purpose except freedom, no goal except a willingness to see how such encounters go and to abide by the outcome. It has no purpose except to make life easier for poets and revolutionaries while seeing to it that they make life harder for others only by words, and not deeds. It is a society whose hero is the strong poet and the revolutionary because it recognizes that it is what it is, has the morality it has, speaks the

language it does, not because it approximates the will of God or the nature of man but because certain poets and revolutionaries of the past spoke as they did. (60–61)

Rorty brings into focus the figure of the liberal ironist by comparing it with Foucault (an ironist who is not a liberal) and with Habermas (a liberal who is not an ironist). In the case of Foucault there is an exclusive emphasis on self-realization, self-enjoyment. Foucault is unwilling to consider the advantages and improvements of liberal societies because he is much more concerned with the ways in which these societies still prevent this process of self-creation. In many cases they have even imposed upon their members increased controls, which were unknown in premodern societies. Rorty's main disagreement with Foucault is that, in his view, it is not necessary to create a new "we"; "we liberals" is enough. With Habermas the situation is the opposite. For him it is essential that a democratic society's self-image have an element of universalism, which is to be obtained through what he calls a process of domination-free communication. He tries to maintain—even if through a radical recasting—a bridge with the rationalistic foundation of the Enlightenment. So, Rorty's disagreement with Foucault is essentially political, whereas with Habermas it is purely philosophical.

Finally, we should consider for our purposes two possible objections to Rorty's liberal utopia, which he tries to answer. The first is that the abandonment of the metaphysical grounding of liberal societies will deprive them of a social glue that is indispensable for the continuation of free institutions. The second is that it is not possible—from a psychological point of view—to be a liberal ironist and, at the same time, not to have some metaphysical beliefs about the nature of human beings. Rorty's answer to the first objection is that society is pulled together not by any philosophical grounding but by common vocabularies and common hopes. The same objection was made in the past about the disastrous social effects that would derive from the masses' loss of religious beliefs, and the prophecy proved to be wrong. The answer to the second objection is that there is something to it. Ironists have been essentially elitist and have not contributed excessively to the improvement of the community. The redescription in which they engage frequently leads to attack on the most cherished values of people and to their humiliation. On top of that, though the metaphysicians also engage in redescriptions, they have the advantage over ironists in that they at least give people something they claim to be true in nature, a new faith to which they can adhere. But here Rorty says that the primary difficulty is that people are demanding from ironist philosophers something that philosophy cannot give: answers to questions such as "Why not be cruel?" or "Why be kind?" The expectation that a *theoretical* answer can be given is simply the result of a metaphysical lag. In a postphilosophical era it is the narratives that perform the function of creating those values:

Within an ironist culture . . . it is the disciplines which specialize in thick description of the private and idiosyncratic which are assigned this job. In particular, novels and ethnographies which sensitize one to the pain of those who do not speak our language must do the job which demonstrations of a common human nature were supposed to do. (97)

II

I am in agreement with a great deal of Rorty's analysis, especially with his pragmatism and with the account that he gives of what is happening in contemporary theory. I certainly subscribe to his rejection of any metaphysical grounding of the social order and with his critique of Habermas. Finally, I also endorse his defense of the liberal democratic framework. However, I think that there is in his "liberal utopia" something that simply does not work. And I do not think that it is a matter of detail or incompletion but rather that it is an internal inconsistency of his "ideal society."

Let us start with his characterization of liberal society as a type of social arrangement in which persuasion substitutes for force. My main difficulty is that I cannot establish between the two as sharp a distinction as Rorty does. Of course in one sense the distinction *is* clear: in persuasion there is an element of consensus, whereas in force there is not. But the question that remains is to what extent in persuasion/consensus there is not an ingredient of force. What is it to persuade? Except in the extreme case of proving something to somebody in an algorithmic way, we are engaged in an operation that involves making somebody change her opinion without any ultimate rational foundation. Rorty quite correctly limits the domain of reason to the interior of any particular language game, but the difficulty subsists, because language games are not absolutely closed universes and, as a consequence, decisions within them have to be made that are undecidable by the system of rules that define the structure of the game. I agree with Rorty/Davidson that recognition of this fact does not justify describing the decision as irrational, and that the whole distinction between rational and irrational is of little use. But what I want to point out is something different: it is that a decision to be made under those conditions is inevitably going to include an element of force. Let us take Davidson's example of somebody who wants to reform herself and decides to suppress a desire—e.g., an alcoholic who decides to stop drinking. From the point of view of the desire there is only repression—that is, force. And this argument can be generalized. Let us consider various possible situations:

Situation A. I am confronted with the need to choose between several possible courses of action, and the structure of the language game that I am playing is indifferent to them. After having evaluated the situation, I conclude that there is no obvious candidate for my decision but I nevertheless make *one* choice. It is clear that in this case I have repressed the alternative courses of action.

Situation B. I want to persuade somebody to change his opinion. Since the belief I want to inculcate in him is not the Hegelian truth of the opposed belief that he actually has, I do not want to develop his belief but to *cancel it out of existence*. Again, force. Let us suppose that I succeed in my efforts. In that case he has been *converted* to my belief. But the element of force is always there. All I have done is convince my friend that by killing his belief he will become my ally. Persuasion, consequently, structurally involves force.

Situation C. There are two possible courses of action and two groups of people are split about which to follow. As the two courses of action are equally possible within the structure of the situation, the differend can only be solved by force. Of course this element of force will be actualized in many different ways: either by one group persuading the other (and we are back to situation B); or through a system of rules accepted by both parties to settle the differend (a vote, for instance); or by the *ultima ratio*. But the important point to see is that the element of force is going to be present in all cases.

Clearly the kind of society that Rorty prefers is that in which the third solution to situation C is excluded, but this still presents various difficulties. The first is that it is simply not possible to oppose force and persuasion since persuasion is one form of force. The discussion is thus displaced to an analysis of the way in which force is organized in society and of the types of force that are acceptable in a liberal society. The second problem is that the element of physical force cannot be eliminated even in the most free society. I doubt that Rorty would advocate persuasion as an adequate method for dealing with a rapist. And strikes, or student sit-ins — which are perfectly legitimate actions in a free society — try to achieve their goals not only through persuasion but also by forcing their antagonists to surrender to violence. There are, of course, many intermediate cases.

For the same reasons I tend to deal in a way different from Rorty with the distinction between reform and revolution. In my view, the problem is to displace the terrain that made the distinction possible. For the classical idea of revolution involves not only the dimension of violence that Rorty underscores but also the idea that this violence has to be directed toward a very specific end, which was to give a *new foundation* to the social order. Now, from this point of view I am a reformist, not because my social aims are limited but simply because I do not believe that society has such a thing as a foundation. No doubt Rorty would agree with me on this point. Even the events that in the past *have been called* revolutions were only the overdetermination of a multiplicity of reforms that cover vast aspects of society but by no means the totality of them. The idea of turning the whole society upside down does not make any sense. (Which does not mean that many ugly things were not committed in the attempt to perform this impossible operation.) But if, on the one hand, I am trying to relocate revolution within reform, on the other hand I am very much in favor of reintroducing the dimension of violence within reform. A world in which reform takes place without violence is not a world in which I would like to live. It could be either an absolutely unidimensional society, in which one hundred percent of the population would agree with any single reform, or a society in which the decisions would be made by an army of social engineers with the backing of the rest of the population. Any reform involves changing the status quo, and in most cases this will hurt existing interests. The process of reform is a process of struggles, not a process of quiet piecemeal engineering. And there is here nothing to regret. It is in this active process of struggle that human abilities—new language games—are created. Could we for instance think what the workers' identity would have been without the active struggles with which they were involved during the first stages of industrial societies? Certainly many of the workers' abilities that will be essential to the process of democratization of Western societies would not have developed. And the same, of course, can be said of any other social force. Thus, the radical democratic "utopia" that I would like to counterpose to Rorty's liberal one does not preclude antagonisms and social division but, on the contrary, considers them as constitutive of the social.

So, in my view Rorty has based his argument on certain types of polarizations—persuasion/force, reform/violence-revolution—that are not only simplistic but also inconsistent because the role of the goodies presupposes the presence, inside it, of baddies. Any theory about power in a democratic society has to be a theory about the forms of power that are compatible with democracy, not about the elimination of power. And this is the result not of any particular persistence of a form of domination but of the very fact that society, as Rorty knows well, is not structured as a jigsaw puzzle and that consequently it is impossible to avoid the collision of different demands and language games with each other. Let us take the case of recent debates in America concerning pornography. Various feminist groups have argued that pornography offends women—something with which I could not agree more. But some of these groups have gone so far as to ask for legislation permitting any woman to take to court the publishers of pornographic material and advertisements. This has raised the objection—which I also share—that such actions would create a climate of intimidation that could affect freedom of expression. Where should the line be drawn between what is pornographic and what is artistic expression, for instance? Obviously a balance has to be established between antagonistic demands. But it is important to stress that the balance is not going to be the result of having found a point at which both demands harmonize with each other—in which case we would be back to the jigsaw puzzle theory. No, the antagonism of the two demands is, in that context, ineradicable, and the balance consists of limiting the effects of both so that a sort of social equilibrium—something very different from a rational harmonization—can be reached. But in that case the antagonism, though socially regulated and controlled, will subsist under the form of what could be called a "war of position." Each pole of the conflict will have a certain power and will exercise a certain violence over the other pole. The paradoxical corollary of this conclusion is that the existence of violence and antagonism is the very condition of a free society. Antagonism exists because the social is not a plurality of effects radiating from a pregiven center, but is pragmatically constructed from many starting points. But it is precisely because of this, because there is an ontological possibility of clashes and unevenness, that we can speak of freedom. Let us suppose that we move to the opposite hypothesis, the one contained in the classical notion of emanicipation—i.e., a society from which violence and antagonisms have been *entirely* eliminated. In this society we only enjoy the Spinozan freedom of being conscious of necessity. This is a first paradox of a free community: that which constitutes its condition of impossibility (violence) constitutes at the same time its condition of possibility. Particular forms of oppression can be eliminated, but freedom exists only insofar as the achievement of a total freedom is an ever-receding horizon. A totally free society and a totally determined society would be, as I have argued elsewhere, exactly the same. I think that the reason Rorty is not entirely aware of these antinomies is the result of his insufficient theorization of what is involved in the notion of "persuasion" and of the total opposition that he has established between "persuasion" and "force."

III

Persuasion is an essentially impure notion. One cannot persuade without the other of persuasion—that is, force. One can speak of the force of persuasion, but one would never say that one has been persuaded of the correctness of the Pythagorean theorem. The latter is simply *shown*, without any need for persuasion. But one cannot say either that persuasion is simply *reducible* to force. Persuasion is the terrain of what Derrida would call a "hymen." It is the point in which the "reasons" for a belief and the "causes" of the belief constitute an inseparable whole. The adoption of a new paradigm in Kuhnian terms is a good example of what I mean. A multitude of small reasons/causes ranging from theoretical difficulties to technical advances in the tools of scientific research overdetermine each other in determining the transition from normal to revolutionary science. And for reasons that I have explained earlier—and which are also clearly present in some way in Kuhn's account—this transition is not an indifferent and painless abandonment but involves repression of other possibilities: it is the result of a struggle. This is obviously more clearly visible when we refer to the politico-ideological field. Now, as Chantal Mouffe and I have argued in *Hegemony and Socialist Strategy*, there is a name in our political tradition that refers to this peculiar operation called persuasion, which is only constituted through the inclusion, within itself, of its violent opposite: this name is "hegemony."

I refer to our book for all aspects concerning the genealogy of the concept of hegemony from the Russian Social Democrats to Gramsci, for its structural characteristics, and for its forms of theoretical articulation with the project of a radical democracy. Here I want only to underscore some aspects that are relevant to the present discussion. The most important one is that "hegemony" is the discursive terrain in which foundationalism began disintegrating in the history of Marxism. What had been presented so far as a necessary consequence of an endogenous development determined by the contradiction between development of the productive forces and existing relations of production, became, escalating from Lenin to Gramsci, the result of a contingent process of political articulation in an open ensemble whose elements had purely relational identities. That is, History (with a capital H) was not a valid object of discourse because it did not correspond to any a priori unified object. The only thing we had was the discontinuous succession of hegemonic blocs, which was not governed by any rationally graspable logic — neither teleological nor dialectical nor causal. As in the relation between the desire that I want to suppress — in Davidson's example — and the decision to suppress it, there is no internal connection at all. On the other hand, there is here an important dialectic to detect between necessity and contingency. If each of the elements intervening in a hegemonic bloc had an identity of its own, its relations with all the others would be merely contingent; but if, on the contrary, the identity of each element is contingent upon its relations with the others, those relations are absolutely necessary if the identity is going to be maintained.

Now the problem to be discussed is the internal logic of this hegemonic operation that underlies the process of persuasion. We will approach it by bringing into the analysis various devices that are thinkable as a result of the transformations that have taken place in contemporary theory. Let us start with the Wittgensteinian example of the rule governing the sequence of a numerical series. I say 1, 2, 3, 4 and ask a friend to continue it: the spontaneous answer would be to say 5, 6, 7, and so on. But I can say that the series I have in mind is not that but 1, 2, 3, 4, 9, 10, 11, 12, et cetera. My friend thinks that he has now understood and proceeds accordingly, but I can say that the series is still not what I had in mind, and so on. The rule governing the series can be indefinitely changed. Everything depends, as Lewis Carroll would put it, on who is in command. Now let us slightly change the example. Let us suppose that we are speaking of a game in which player A starts a series and player B has to continue it the way he wants, providing that there is some visible regularity. Now, when it is again A's turn, he has to invent a new rule that takes as its starting point the series as it has been left by B, and so on. In the end the loser is the one who finds the whole business so complicated that he is unable to imagine a new rule. The corollaries that follow

from this example are the following: (a) that there is no ultimate rule: it can always be subverted; (b) that since an indefinite number of players can come to
participate in the game, the rule governing the series is essentially threatened — it
is, to use Rorty's expression, *radically contingent*; (c) that the identity of each of
the individual figures within the series is entirely relational; it is only given by its
structural position within the rule that is at that moment hegemonizing the series,
and it will change with the formulation of a new rule. I think this is important
because the process of persuasion is frequently presented as if somebody who has
a belief A is presented with a belief B and the suggestion of moving from one to
the other. Things never happen this way. What happens is rather that new elements enter into the picture and that the old rule is unable to hegemonize them —
if, for instance, an apparently chaotic series of numbers is introduced in our series and the challenge is to find a coherent rule that will be compatible with the
new state of affairs. Very frequently the new rule is accepted, not because it is
liked in itself, but just because it is *a* rule, because it introduces a principle of
coherence and intelligibility in an apparent chaos. In the confused Italian situation of the early 1920s many liberals accepted fascism, not because they particularly liked it, but because an explosive social situation existed that was both
unthinkable and unmanageable within the framework of the traditional political
system, and fascism appeared as the *only* coherent discourse that could deal with
the new chaotic events. And if liberalism had wanted — which it did not — to
present itself as an alternative hegemonic discourse articulating the new elements, it could have done so only by transforming itself. Between the liberalism
of 1905 and the liberalism of 1922 there are only "family resemblances." This is
because, among other reasons, the latter had to be antifascist and this involved
dealing with a new series of problems that radically transformed the discursive
field. This is the reason I do not agree with Rorty's assertion that we can be *just*
liberals; that our "we" has reached a point that does not require any further
transformation. Even if we want to continue being liberals we will *always* have to
be something more. Liberalism can only exist as a hegemonic attempt in this process of articulation — as a result of the radically relational character of all identity.
Here I think that Rorty has not been historicist enough.

This is also the point — moving now from Wittgenstein to Derrida — in which
deconstruction becomes central for a theory of politics. Derrida has shown the
essential vulnerability of every context:

> Every sign, linguistic or not linguistic, spoken or written (in the current
> sense of this opposition), in a small or large unit, can be *cited*, put
> between quotation marks; in so doing it can break with every given
> context, engendering an infinitude of new contexts in a manner which is
> absolutely illimitable. This does not imply that the mark is valid outside
> of a context, but on the contrary that there are only contexts without
> any center of absolute anchorage (*ancrage*). This citationality, this

duplication or duplicity, this iterability of the mark is neither an accident
nor an anomaly, it is that (normal/abnormal) without which a mark
could not even have a function called "normal." What would a mark be
that could not be cited? Or one whose origins would not get lost along
the way? ("Signature," 12)

Now, what is this saying if not that all context is essentially vulnerable and open,
that the fact that one of the possibilities rather than the others has been chosen is
a purely *contingent* fact? If the choice is not *determined* by the structure, it is
down to the bottom a hegemonic operation, an essentially *political* decision.

Let us go back, with these distinctions in mind, to Rorty's text. The first aspect of his liberal utopia I would take issue with is his sharp division between the
public and the private. It is not, of course, that I want to return to some "grand
theory" that would embrace both. The reason for my disagreement is exactly the
opposite: Rorty sees as necessarily united many things that for me are radically
discontinuous and held together only through contingent articulations. Is the
realm of personal self-realization really a *private* realm? It would be so if that
self-realization took place in a neutral medium in which individuals could seek
unimpeded the fulfillment of their own aims. But this medium is, of course, a
myth. A woman searching for her self-realization will find obstacles in the form
of male-oriented rules that will limit her *personal* aspirations and possibilities.
The feminist struggles tending to change those rules will constitute a collective
"we" *different* from the "we" of the abstract public citizenship, but the space
that these struggles create — remember the motto "the personal is political" —
will be no less a communitarian and public space than the one in which political
parties intervene and in which elections are fought. And the same can be said, of
course, of any struggle that begins as a result of the existence of social norms,
prejudices, regulations, and so forth that frustrate the self-realization of an individual. I see the *strength* of a democratic society in the multiplication of these
public spaces and its *condition* in the recognition of their plurality and autonomy.
This recognition is based on the essential *discontinuity* existing between those
social spaces, and the essential character of these discontinuities makes possible
its exact opposite: the contingent-hegemonic articulation among them in what
could be called a global sense of community, a certain democratic common
sense. We see here a second paradox of community: it has to be *essentially* una-
chievable to become pragmatically possible. So, what about the private? It is a
residual category, limited to those aspects of our activity in which our objectives
are not interfered with by any structural social barrier, in which their achievement does not require the constitution of any struggling community, of any
"we." So, as we see, the classical terms of the problem are displaced: it is no
longer a question of preventing a public space from encroaching upon that of private individuals, given that the public spaces have to be constituted in order to

achieve individual aims. But the condition for a democratic society is that these public spaces have to be plural: a democratic society is, of course, incompatible with the existence of only *one* public space. What we should have is a multiple "civic republicanism."

As is clear, my idea of a democratic society is different in central respects from Rorty's liberal utopia. Rorty's utopia consists of a public space limited — as for all good liberals — to minimal functions and a private sphere in which individual agents seek their own ends. This system can certainly be reformed and improved, but one has the impression that such improvements are like improving a machine by designing a better model, not the result of struggles. Antagonism and violence do not play either a positive or a negative role, simply because they are entirely absent from the picture. For me, a radically democratic society is one in which a plurality of public spaces, constituted around specific issues and demands, and strictly autonomous of each other, instills in their members a civic sense that is a central ingredient of their identity *as* individuals. Despite the plurality of these spaces, or, rather, as a consequence of it, a diffuse democratic culture is created, which gives the community its specific identity. Within this community, the liberal institutions — parliament, elections, division of powers — are maintained, but these are *one* public space, not *the* public space. Not only is antagonism not excluded from a democratic society, but it is the very condition of its institution.

For Rorty the three words "bourgeois, liberal democracy" constitute an indivisible whole; for me there is between them only a contingent articulation. As a socialist I am prepared to fight against capitalism for the hegemony of liberal institutions; and as a believer in the latter, I am prepared to do my best to make them compatible with the whole field of democratic public spaces. I see this compatibility, however, as a hegemonic construction, not as something granted from the beginning. I think that a great deal of twentieth-century history can be explained by the dislocations in the articulation of the three components just mentioned. Liberal institutions (let alone capitalism) have fared badly in Third World countries, and the record of the attempt to articulate socialism and democracy (if attempt it can be called) in the countries of the Eastern bloc is simply appalling. Though my preference is for a liberal-democratic-socialist society, it is clear to me that if I am forced under given circumstances to choose one of the three, my preference will always be for democracy. (For instance, if in a Third World country I have to choose between, on the one hand, a corrupt and repressive liberal regime, in which elections are a farce manipulated by clientelistic gangs, with no participation of the masses; and, on the other, a nationalistic military regime that tends toward social reform and the self-organization of the masses, my preference will be for the latter. All my experience shows that, while in some cases the second type of regime can lead — with many difficulties — to an increasing liberalization of its institutions, the same process does not take place in the first case: it is just a blind alley.)

IV

Finally, I want to address the two possible objections to his argument that Rorty raises (see *supra*), and his answers to them. Regarding the first objection, I think that Rorty is entirely correct and I have nothing to add. But in the case of the second objection, I feel that Rorty's answer is unnecessarily defensive and that a much better argument can be made. I would formulate it in this way. The question is whether the abandonment of universalism undermines the foundation of a democratic society. My answer is yes, I grant the whole argument. Without a universalism of sorts — the idea of *human* rights, for instance — a truly democratic society is impossible. But in order to assert this it is not at all necessary to muddle through the Enlightenment's rationalism or Habermas's "domination-free communication." It is enough to recognize that democracy needs universalism while asserting, at the same time, that universalism is one of the vocabularies, one of the language games, which was constructed at some point by social agents and which has become a more and more central part of our values and our culture. It is a *contingent* historical product. It originated in religious discourse (all men are equal before God), was brought down to this world by the Enlightenment, and has been generalized to wider and wider social relations by the democratic revolution of the last two centuries.

A historicist recasting of universalism has, I would think, two main political advantages over its metaphysical version, and these, far from weakening it, help to reinforce and to radicalize it. The first is that it has a liberating effect: human beings will begin seeing themselves more and more as the exclusive authors of their world. The historicity of Being will become more apparent. If people think that God or Nature has made the world as it is, they will tend to consider their fate inevitable. But if the Being of the world that they inhabit is only the result of the contingent discourses and vocabularies that constitute it, they will tolerate their fate with less patience and will stand a better chance of becoming *political* "strong poets." The second advantage is that the perception of the contingent character of universalist values will make us all more conscious of the dangers that threaten them and of their possible extinction. If we happen to believe in those values, the consciousness of their historicity will not make us more indifferent to them, but, on the contrary, will make us more responsible citizens, more ready to engage in their defense. Historicism, in this way, helps those who believe in those values. As for those who *do not* believe in them, no rationalist argument will ever have the slightest effect.

This leads me to a last point. This double effect — increasing the freeing of

human beings through a more assertive image of their capacities, increasing social responsibility through the consciousness of the historicity of Being—is the
most important possibility, a radically *political* possibility, that contemporary
thought is opening to us. The metaphysical discourse of the West is coming to an
end, and philosophy in its dusk has performed, through the great names of the
century, a last service for us: the deconstruction of its own terrain and the creation of the conditions for its own impossibility. Let us think, for instance, of
Derrida's undecidables. Once undecidability has reached the ground itself, once
the organization of a certain camp is governed by a hegemonic decision—
hegemonic because it is not objectively determined, because different decisions
were also possible—the realm of philosophy comes to an end and the realm of
politics begins. This realm will be inhabited by a different type of discourse, by
discourses such as Rorty's "narratives," which tend to *construct* the world on
the grounds of a radical undecidability. But I do not like the name "ironist"—
which evokes all kinds of playful images—for this political strong poet. On the
contrary, someone who is confronted with Auschwitz and has the moral strength
to admit the contingency of her own beliefs instead of seeking refuge in religious
or rationalistic myths is, I think, a profoundly heroic and tragic figure. This will
be a hero of a new type who has still not been entirely created by our culture, but
one whose creation is absolutely necessary if our time is going to live up to its
most radical and exhilarating possibilities.

Laclau's and Mouffe's
Secret Agent

Paul Smith

I want here to address some of the questions arising from Ernesto Laclau's and Chantal Mouffe's book, *Hegemony and Socialist Strategy* (1985). This book has, of course, been a central text for the discussions of community in the context of the conference to which this essay was originally a contribution. The book has also been of particular relevance to my own work on the categories of "subject" and "agent" in the human sciences, as well as constituting a major and controversial intervention into the political debate on the left in Europe and America. My discussion here will try to do two things in particular in relation to this book and the issues it has raised for theoretical work on the left. First, I want to emblematize my sense of the importance of Laclau's and Mouffe's work by offering some kind of defense of it, against some of the many questions it has provoked in various forums over the last several years. Specifically, many critics have seen Laclau's and Mouffe's work as departing so far from recognizable Marxist paradigms that it has landed up embracing some form of liberalism; this charge of liberalism is what I will want to question, as it were on their behalf.

I want also to stress, however, that this will be only a partial defense. Since the original composition of this essay, and thus since the date of the conference at which these issues arose, I think I have been able to see more nearly some of the problems with Laclau's and Mouffe's book. These problems were perhaps hidden in the first flush of my enthusiasm for a work that appeared to be a radical departure for leftist thinking. My second task, however, is to adumbrate what for me turned out to be the first signs of such problems, and to point to the area where I now feel a critique of Laclau and Mouffe must begin. That is, I want to look at Laclau's and Mouffe's notion of the *subject* of radical democracy and suggest that this notion can be—indeed, needs to be—discerned further in order to locate an *agent* of radical democracy. My initial proposition is that Laclau's and Mouffe's agent of radical democracy is as yet a secret one, and that this is a problem arising from their stress on the destructuring, or decompositional, aspects of poststructuralism's theories of subjectivity. Despite their own caveat that "analysis [of the subject] cannot simply remain at the moment of dispersion" (*Hegemony*, 117), I think they have not yet sufficiently entertained the idea that, in order to give agency to the poststructuralist subject, it might well be necessary to pass beyond the very terms of the subjectivity debate as posed in poststructuralism.

While Laclau's and Mouffe's work obviously is heavily contingent upon the various modes of poststructuralist theory that they install at its surface, and while most commentary on it has been concerned to discuss its "post-Marxism," it might be useful to address it from another angle, or indeed from the perspective of an altogether different disciplinary field. That is, *Hegemony and Socialist Strategy* can perhaps be usefully considered as arising from a specific tradition in contemporary social theory itself. In particular, their work seems to me to contribute to the elaboration of that kind of social theory that has recently abandoned, or tried to abandon, all essentializing and totalizing notions of the social whole, along with the universalist tendencies of much of our thought inherited from the European Enlightenment. One of the authors of such social theory is Alain Touraine, and I will be referring quite often here to his most recently available work in English, *Return of the Actor* (1988). Part of the function of such work as his has been (contrary to the complaints of many of its detractors) not the purely negative function of dismissing Marxism, but the more positive function of engaging with the principles of energy in the social that have begun to find expression in what we now often call the new social movements. Notably, Touraine has had much to say about Solidarity in Poland, and about the nature of the social upheaval that has recently taken place in Eastern Europe. It seems to me that much of the change in Eastern Europe is indeed susceptible of explanation in terms of his analysis of Solidarity and his attempts to relate it and similar movements to what is variously called the postmodern era, the postindustrial age, or what Touraine himself has called "the programmed society."

I think it makes some sense to claim that the central moment in the elaboration of such nontotalizing social theory—and thus a basis for a theory of radical democracy such as Laclau's and Mouffe's—is the decision to privilege politics itself, if not as a wholly autonomous realm, then at least as unleashed from primary determination by, and relieved of merely secondary status in relation to, the categories of the economic and the ideological. This is, of course, precisely the move that makes many of the critics of their work so hostile and nervous. Under the guise of, as it were, protecting or revindicating various aspects of Marxist thought, these critics might well be simply refusing the task that Laclau's and Mouffe's work demands—the promotion of politics to the everyday and center stage, the consideration of politics as primary. There is probably little need to reiterate here Laclau's and Mouffe's argument for this primacy, except to point out that in a very real sense it is derived from Marx himself. Laclau in an earlier work has reminded us that for Marx "class struggle is only that which constitutes classes as such" (*Politics and Ideology,* 106). In other words, what are often thought of as presignified social positions are the result of, and not the prerequisite to, political struggle and the negotiation of interests.

Laclau and Mouffe will eventually carry that early insistence much further, to the point of arguing that "the economic space itself is structured as a political space" first and foremost ("Post-Marxism," 94). In that emphasis, they agree with Touraine, whose similar kinds of theories of radical democracy actually tend to devolve upon his definition of the economic as only "the object of intervention of society upon itself," and thus as not the primary determinant of the social (*Return,* 104).

But in itself, proposing the primacy of politics in the place of theories of determinism might also appear as exactly an embracing of the liberal tradition as we have known it since the Enlightenment; and this is where Laclau and Mouffe sometimes seem vulnerable—here, rather than in relation to the more simplistic charge that they have abandoned Marxism (a charge that seems especially useless when most of their critics on that score appear to be able to give no pressing reasons why Marxism should be preserved except for its own sake, through a kind of faith in its theoretical purity). The sense we generally have of liberalism is tied exactly to its origins in Enlightenment thought and to the bourgeois revolutions of the eighteenth century. And so, when they insist on the importance of that history in their championing of the traditions and discourses of egalitarianism, Laclau and Mouffe open themselves to the interpretation that they have simply assimilated themselves into the tradition that we now call liberalism.

However, if we come at their work as I suggested before (through its relation to social and political theory), I think its distance from liberalism can be demonstrated quite easily. It is possible to analyze, for the sake of argument, the whole field of the liberal tradition by reference to Isaiah Berlin's well-known characterization. Liberalism is basically constituted in two huge strands of thinking, which are both internally contested and which contest with each other. Indeed, their contestation in both these senses defines political debate, not just on the terrain of social theory, but in the political institutions of our Euro-American tradition. Berlin (*Four Essays on Liberty*) identifies these strands as supporting notions either of positive liberty or of negative liberty. Negative liberty does not construe any set of objective or teleological notions of the good and instead depends, after Hobbes, on the ideal of unimpeded motion for the individual subject. Positive liberty on the other hand proposes a codified or rule-bound ideal by which the subject's rights and responsibilities are civically defined and indeed circumscribed. It is the place or the definition of the subject that is of interest here when considering Laclau's and Mouffe's departure from the liberal tradition. They subscribe to neither of the two ideologies of the subject available in liberalism. In the first, the subject is as it were a "natural" subject whose freedom is the absence of civic or institutional impediment. In the second, the subject is a "civic" subject whose freedom is willfully realized in civic institutions. In both these humanist versions, however, the subject is assumed either to be motivated primarily by self-interest or to be primarily definable in terms of a relationship to civic institutions. For Laclau and Mouffe, the definition of the subject in these alternative, but complementary, ways—in terms of either a positive or a negative liberty—is not only proper to liberalism but is also its very problematic. Their work seems to me to have been predicated upon a refusal of those notions of subjectivity without which liberalism does not exist.

To reject or redefine the traditional humanist subject of liberalism necessitates a rethinking of the notions of liberty and freedom for which that subject has been made the support or bearer. For liberalism, the subject's freedom is defined relative to the progressive or evolutionary establishment of universal norms, ideas of the good, the totality of the social, and so on. There has been in social theory, however, a line of thought that abandons the belief in the possibility either of constructing a typology of the social, or of pursuing any sense of the evolutionary progress of the social. Rather, this tradition says, the social should be analyzed exclusively from the point of view of change. This claim can in fact take a liberalist tinge when it silently advocates a simple evolutionary passage from societies of control to societies of individual freedom. But a less committedly liberal version would see the need to analyze the social as the self-sufficient network of its processes captured in overdetermined social relations; that is, the place of the production of power is the social itself, and its measure is the diachronic insistence, or preeminence, of social relations themselves over institutions, whether they are political, economic, or whatever.

Laclau and Mouffe seem to me to belong clearly to this latter, antiliberal tendency. Often the insights that arise from this way of thinking depend, in the same way as Laclau himself depends in his earlier work (*Politics and Ideology*), upon a critique of the ideological nature of any appeal to progress-as-norm. Such critiques themselves often arise, not by a direct critique of the Enlightenment, for example, but rather through the lessons of alternative or oppositional nationalisms, which in the twentieth century have regularly opposed the universalist values of the North and put forward very specific claims for self-determination that fundamentally challenge and struggle with the enforcement of the liberal progress-as-norm.

Even at home, liberalism has been undermined by the increasing instability of one of its underlying assumptions: the assumption of indefinite growth in production. Optimistically (and crudely), one might think of the Thatcher/Kohl/

Reagan years as the final huge effort to reinstall faith in that ideology. But faced with ever more discernible limits to growth and with the ever more regular effects of depredations produced by the North's insistence that it still can happen, we are at a historical point where ideologies of norms, progress, and growth are not only compromised by their own contradictions, but increasingly often understood to be so compromised. The recent marked increase in the attention paid to ecological concerns by the agents of capital themselves is perhaps the most overt signal of this.

The rejection of the subject of liberalism is perhaps an inevitable corollary of the exposure of the increasing inadequacy of some of the Enlightenment ideologies that have traditionally underpinned capitalism. If we can define liberalism as having established within politics the supposed self-grounding of a subject that will pursue its own interests, and that these interests are themselves posited as essentially in the service of progress toward the universal norm or the universal good, this conception of the political begins to unravel with the removal of its founding subject. The political comes to be defined in a way much closer to what Touraine suggests when he claims that now,

> instead of looking at ourselves as lords and masters of nature and the world, we feel that we face choices that are not reducible to quantitative transformations but rather are concerned with elaborating different relations between human beings and their environment as well as among human beings themselves. We are replacing the idea of indefinite progress with that of a choice, by particular collectivities, of equally particular life-styles and social organization (*Return*, 114).

This kind of perspective, which Laclau and Mouffe would appear to share, takes up a huge distance from the liberal tradition even when what is at stake is the notion of democracy itself. The kind of perspective that they and Touraine put forward has virtually nothing in common with contemporary liberalist views of democracy, from Benjamin Barber's Rousseauian argument in *Strong Democracy* (1984) for the strengthening of democracy by a massive extension of political machinery, through to Norberto Bobbio's version of representationalism in *The Future of Democracy* (1987)—which looks more to me like a covert defense of Montesquieu's ideal monarchy than anything else.

There are, however, some important differences between Laclau and Mouffe and Touraine. Not the least of these is Laclau's and Mouffe's insistence that all social argumentation must be groundless, that there are no essential categories in politics. For their version of radical democracy, political argument itself must increase in importance, since political argument is what actually constructs social relations and thus political reality. However, for them this argumentation is necessarily deprived of decidability even as it becomes a more and more crucial component of political action. Obviously, Laclau's and Mouffe's embracing of this epistemological groundlessness can easily be understood as pointing toward an impossibility of social and political action, or to what used to be called quietism. I think this is what happens in the work of some others influenced by Laclau and Mouffe: for example, a lot of the writing in cultural studies on postmodernism in the United States or, in a very different mode and with a more ambivalent relation to Laclau and Mouffe, the journal *Marxism Today* in Britain.

In light of the threat of political undecidabilty that is always a specter for me in reading Laclau and Mouffe, I would want to add a different kind of emphasis, one that can be found in Touraine's discussions of the same kinds of problem. For Touraine, there are always specific material stakes, definable referents, in political argumentation. He agrees that these stakes do not constitute power as such but rather are matters of self-determination, an energy or a movement, a turning of energy around the attempt to orientate what he calls "historicity." By "historicity" he means the actual enactment of political processes whereby a lived culture comes to be meaningful for the agent—culture seen there as "a set of resources and models that social actors seek to manage and to control" (*Return*, 8). Touraine's careful consideration and definition of historicity seems to me to have the advantage of turning immediately to a materialist and institutional notion of culture, and even allows that new hegemonic blocs will eventually find themselves having to confront the question of the state. In this I think Touraine differs radically from Laclau and Mouffe, and I'll return to the issue a little later.

For now, if the distance from liberalism in Laclau and Mouffe can be measured in part around their conception of the subject, it is to that conception that I want to turn since, as was obviously to be expected, the distancing itself brings up many other problems, especially around the explanation of how situations of subordination are turned to antagonism and hegemonic articulation. The subject is crucially involved there, and in some ways the questions one must ask about its role are little different from the ones that need to be asked about the by now classic dilemmas of social theory when it poses the problem of how, by what mechanisms and logics, subject and structure meet.

Laclau and Mouffe attempt to explain the articulation of subject and structure through the Lacanian view of the construction of the subject in language; specifically, they deploy a version of subjectivity derived from Lacan's description of how linguistic meaning is anchored at *points de capiton* in the midst of the free flow of signifiers. The image of the *point de capiton* refers to the moment of condensation whereby, as Lacan puts it, signifiers fall to the rank of the signified. It seems to me somewhat problematic that Laclau and Mouffe should use this image to describe a provisional halting of the very indeterminacy that is crucial to their account of the social; that is, having claimed that they see the social as having no fixed ground, here they deploy a Lacanian account of how social fixity actually takes hold. In their view, the *point de capiton* halts indeterminacy and permits the subject to partake in political choice and activity by articulating itself around what they call the empty signifier of "rights" or "democracy." But we might recall that for Lacan this is the moment of the imposition of the law of culture, and thus if the notion of rights or democracy or whatever is constituted at a *point de capiton*, then it is in fact not a signifier, still less an empty signifier, but a *signified*, fully implicated into the ideological and historical discourses of a particular culture.

Quite apart from the fact that this Lacanian model introduces some theoretical contradiction for the indeterminacy thesis that has underpinned much of their work, there is perhaps a more serious problem that Laclau and Mouffe overlook here. That is, they seem to assume that the Lacanian explanation of subjective captation into the symbolic can equally act as an explanation of the articulation of social blocs; or in other words, *they appear to take for granted that the construction of the subject is in some way the same as the construction of a social/political discourse.* Here we have a rather too hasty projection of the Lacanian theory of the subject's construction onto what I would claim is the altogether different issue of collective articulation and agency around particular discourses (rights, etc.). It is a startling lapse, in my view, for theorists so sophisticated as Laclau and Mouffe to blithely draw a direct analogy between the construction of these two orders.

Those two criticisms arising from Laclau's and Mouffe's use of a Lacanian model might provide the starting point for a reexamination of their notion of subjectivity. As I have suggested, the difficulties that arise from their use of this model have something to do with their apparent confusion between signifiers and signifieds in the Lacanian schema, and this confusion has certain other consequences through which it might be possible to reexamine some of the conclusions of their work. In particular, if subjects articulate themselves or are articulated around particular signifiers that are empty, it would be incumbent upon any theorist of hegemonic formation to present some account of why and how particular discourses are foregrounded or found appropriate. In other words, a historical characterization and genealogy of such discourses would be necessary. Laclau's and Mouffe's theory at this point does not provide such accounts. The reason for this is in part indicated by Laclau's article "Metaphor and Social Antagonisms" (1988) and his apparent view of the relation of history to discursive formations. There Laclau separates out the paradigmatic and syntagmatic axes of discourse, suggesting that "if difference exists only in the diachronic succession of the syntagmatic pole, equivalence exists at the paradigmatic pole" ("Metaphor," 256). It is, I think, an elementary structuralist error to assign difference and diachrony to one discursive pole, the syntagmatic, but not to the other, the paradigmatic. I would suggest instead that the paradigmatic axis never contains a series of atemporal or ahistorical equivalencies, as Laclau claims, but rather is made up of differentiated elements all with precisely a different *history* that will constrain their attachment to given signifiers. Thus the historicity of discourse is not a function of merely the temporal movement of the syntagmatic. In other words, discourse is not ahistorical, however you cut it.

The problems I am sketching out here are threefold and are far from a mere quibbling over theoretical models. First, Laclau and Mouffe appear to understand the subject's construction in language as a generalizable affair, appropriate as a description of whole social formations. Second, the theoretical models they use seem to compromise their own claims for indeterminacy in the social and lead to a sleight of hand by which a Lacanian moment of *subject*-ion is blurred as a Laclau/Mouffian moment of radical agency. Third, they seem to be able to offer no reason(ing) for the subject's articulation with or within particular discourses and this inability is related to their mistaking of the historical nature of discourse itself. In short, I am suggesting that there is something problematic about Laclau's and Mouffe's dealings with the subject at the level of its intersection with the discursive formations that preexist it. I am not even so much bothered, as someone like Norman Geras (1987) is, by the obvious fact that their much-vaunted indeterminacy thesis is somewhat compromised by the theoretical models they choose at this point (though I happen to think that is right). Rather, I simply want to throw into the argument some different emphases which, I think, ought to have different consequences for the kinds of politics Laclau and Mouffe claim to have elaborated, while still staying very much within their general orbit. Specifically, I want to make a couple of suggestions.

It seems crucial to me that the notion of radical democracy furnish itself with a theory that will take into account the fact that the agent of radical democracy will not automatically emerge from even the most correct forms of discourse theory. (Ironically, I have heard Laclau warn us on several occasions that it is a mistake to assume that the logic of concepts can be transferred directly to the world.) Rather, we need to recognize and help produce the *reason*, or *reason(ing)*, for the agent. In order that the subject of discourses, in Laclau's and Mouffe's sense, might be seen as the active agent of antagonism and thence of hegemony, it must find some *reason* to articulate itself with the social discourses that preexist it or that constitute its history.

My first suggestion toward that end, then, is that the theory of radical democracy needs to consider much more fully the historical dimensions of discourse, and to stress the historical reasons for the centrality of particular discourses such as the discourse of rights, or that of privacy, and so on. I am well aware, of course, that my suggestion here appears to ignore the way in which Mouffe in particular has tried to locate the importance of discourses of egalitarianism within the history of our post-Enlightenment tradition. Hers is a project that one can only endorse. At the same time it is necessary to ask what the theoretical connection is between that historical work and the models of subjectivity and discourse deployed in *Hegemony and Socialist Strategy*. In other words, what can the relationship be between a theory of indeterminacy and the work of historical specificity? Perhaps my problem here is simply a wariness produced by the fact that in our time theses of indeterminacy tend to be somewhat selective, not to say gingerly, about their use of history.

My second suggestion concerns the mechanism by which the mass of overlapping subject positions in which we consist can be described in a way that will avoid reducing subject positions to mere effects of the signified set into relations of equivalency one with the other. I have argued at length in *Discerning the Subject* for what I think such a mechanism might be,[1] under the broad heading of the notion of negativity produced by the contradictions and antagonistic impulses derived from the multiple aims of interpellation (see especially chapter 8). Subject positions seen in this way help provide the clue to how the "subject" articulates with, or invests in, the particular kinds of discursive structures and meanings that preexist it in the social, and help, I think, to conceptualize the "subject's" becoming agent.

I want also to argue that one of the questions around the notion of subjectivity that might benefit from the kinds of amendments I have suggested to Laclau's and Mouffe's theory would be the somewhat vexed question of essentialist subject positions, and/or the whole question of identity. Laclau and Mouffe are, I would say, quite ruthless in their rejection of the principle of identity in politics, and I think this is a mistake, both historically and theoretically. The appeal to identity is in many actually existing contexts and instances a crucial moment in the production of what Laclau and Mouffe want to see as the movement from subordination to antagonism to hegemonic articulation, and yet they appear to reject it utterly. But I think it is true that, even empirically, almost any of the new forms of agency that we might look to in the social fields around us confirms the necessity—and indeed the efficacy—of appeals to identity in both the passage from subordination to antagonism and, to a degree, in the project of hegemonic articulation. We are familiar with the issue perhaps from feminism, or from some parts of green politics—the one with an appeal to the identity and specificity of the feminine, the other with its appeal to the specificity of the natural. In this context, even recourses to notions of class identity should not be ruled out of court prima facie, since the discourse of class is still—that is, historically—an important available discourse in the political field and is thus still an element of our historicity. As Touraine points out, such "appeal[s] to identity [are] first of all a rejection of social roles, a refusal of the social definition of the roles that must be played by the social actor" (*Return*, 75). Such rejections can be explained in my terms as the results of the production of negativity in and by subject positions in the ways that I've mentioned before, and the aspiration to identity is almost always a matter of taking advantage of historically available, and historically laden, *signifieds*. Again quoting Touraine, the appeal to "identity [is] no longer an appeal to a mode of being [as such] but the claim to a specific capacity for action and change" (81).

Touraine of course also quickly concedes the perhaps rather defensive character of this strategy and suggests that identity has an ambiguity: "It can both restore life to collective action *and* lock it up behind the walls of sectarianism" (82). In his view, movements originally based on identity stand little chance of becoming empowered unless articulated with or within what he calls a counteroffensive moment. The process whereby such an articulation might occur is a social and political one, open to strategizing at the level of conscious decision. But the important point, I think, is to learn from the actual internal constitution of the new social agents and their political space; to learn, indeed, that the appeal to identity is often a crucial step in the production of antagonism.

In many ways it seems to me incumbent on Laclau and Mouffe to champion this kind of approach. Indeed, their book's insistent attacks on class and other kinds of identities are actually considerably mollified by Mouffe's comment in another context that "it would, in fact, be wrong to oppose radically the struggles of workers to the struggles of the new social movements, both are efforts to obtain new rights or defend endangered ones. Their common element is thus a fundamental one" ("Hegemony and New Political Subjects," 96). I would agree, and would extend the point, so as to claim that it is necessary to recognize the appeal to the essential, the natural, and so on, as again historically available components of the discourses around which the potential agent might be mobilized. These moments, to quote Touraine once more, are those where "subjects come to an awareness not of their works but of the distance that separates them from a hostile or meaningless order of things, in their desire for freedom and creation" (*Return*, 160).

This brings me to my final point, where I would like to propose that as political "subjects," separated from a hostile or meaningless order of things, we of necessity construct for ourselves some kind of relationship to the representative institution of that order—in particular, the state. Laclau's and Mouffe's work is largely silent about such a relationship except tentatively to suggest that new articulations and blocs and the proliferation of new political spaces will lead to reform in the state as well as civil society. It is true that in their response to Norman Geras they talk of the "consolidation and democratic reform of the liberal State" ("Post-Marxism," 105). But I get the sense that even this is a concession on an issue that they don't really want to talk about. With that in mind, I want quickly, through the work of one of the thinkers behind *Hegemony and Socialist Strategy*—namely, Gramsci—to throw out a couple of questions about that issue of the state.

If, roughly speaking, the principles of hegemony are consent, negotiation, and articulation, then Gramsci is quite right when he recognizes that political power within modernity and its firmly entrenched culture of liberalism could never simply be *seized*, but would rather have to be *built*—pieced together through the transformation of aspirations, values, and practices from a broadly conceived social ground. But it can also be said of Gramsci that his understanding of modernity also relies heavily upon Machiavelli, who claims that the collapse of the medieval world ushers in among other things the necessity of a primarily *pragmatic politics*. In other words, what characterizes modernity is not simply the legitimated existence of plural society but concomitantly the advent of enormous and ruthless structures of power—institutions with which any new hegemonic bloc would eventually have to reckon. Thus while Laclau and Mouffe are perhaps right to argue that Gramsci's predilections for unity and the party are in no way logically necessary and indeed might bear a residue of essentialism, this doesn't necessarily demand the rejection of the idea of the party, an organization of power equipped to counter capital and the state, which represents Gramsci's answer to a question that Laclau's and Mouffe's strategy of hegemony never even addresses: what can be said or done about precisely the superhuman *scale* of the organizations where political power currently resides? And the concomitant question: can conceptions of struggle and power that rely upon the logic of non-necessity and contingency do anything to counter these organizations? For Gramsci (and, I would argue, for us right now) the problem is that while the Western left worries over democracy and allows us rather too easily to imagine that we can after all still do politics and still resist, capitalism and the state become increasingly less democratic, and this raises the question of whether the left's weapons could ever be able to make a dent against the right's fortresses. Gramsci recognizes that the extent and scale of state power (its sheer *force*) would necessitate not only the simultaneous formation of organic hegemonic blocs and an increase in the degree of social democratization at all levels, but also the formation and exercise of an organizational base proportionate in scale to state power and which could directly contend with the state itself. Hence the party, Gramsci's concession to *politics*, a politics that is not just elevated to a prime theoretical position, but that is also seen as a pragmatic issue.

Laclau's and Mouffe's unwillingness to entertain such a compromise, and what is all too readable as their general antipathy to the idea of a party, could be thought of as exaggerated because it too arises from a conflation of ideas that itself is not necessary. They seem to imagine that, because the party has so often been located by most Marxisms at one level or another as the instrument of pre-signified class unity, it can be conceived of *only* as such. Their general hostility to the notion of class as a subject position directly tied to the relations of production entails, therefore, that they reject partyism out of hand. They are in one sense as extreme as their opponents. Where an apologist for Marxism like Ellen Wood assumes that a party is necessary to act for a class, Laclau and Mouffe make the same assumption and then resist it. I should like to ask whether it's not still possible to conceive of a party—as Eduard Bernstein in fact did—as something other than simply the organ of the proletariat and use it to carry out the necessary political tasks to which Gramsci himself had assigned it? Is it not still necessary to entertain such notions in the context where Laclau's and Mouffe's radical democracy promises only a gradualist reform and indeed even a strengthening of state apparatuses (the "consolidation . . . of the liberal State" ["Post-Marxism," 105])?

I end on a question, wanting indeed to stress that the series of questions that this essay has tried to pose are fundamentally friendly ones in that they have assumed a lot of the same ground as, and share certain ambitions with, Laclau's and Mouffe's book. My suggestions and questions have, however, tried to cast some doubt on some of the terms of their view of subjectivity; and, perhaps on a grander scale, I've intimated that the terms of the poststructuralist accounts of the "subject" will have to be surpassed if we are to reach an adequate notion of, or explanation for, the place of the agent in relation to the manifold and variegated structures of power and resistance that we live in. The agent still needs to be flushed out into the open and I suspect will turn out, as in any good espionage story, to be a double agent—in the sense that its construction takes place not only in the new multiplicity of political spaces but also in the historical realm of discourses and institutions: the agent is not a theoretical "subject" but an active actor, and crucially a historical entity among historically laden discourses.[2]

Notes

1. After my practice in that book, I put quotation marks around "subject" in order to signal the project of problematizing that concept on the way to a theory of agency.

2. I'm grateful to Lisa Frank for sharing her extensive knowledge of the texts mentioned here (and of many others).

On the Dialectics of Postdialectical Thinking

Richard Terdiman

In the paper he presented to this colloquium, Jean-François Lyotard told us there was no dialectic. But I want to claim there was a dialectic in what he told us. (I also want to say that I found what he told us moving—*émouvant*—and important.) And I want to make a further point, or point further. Or, with respect, to point Jean-François Lyotard further. And along with him something that I will be calling—with blissful imprecision—poststructuralism.

Poststructuralism's power seems to me rooted in some fundamental paradoxes. Poststructuralism is a fundamentally anti-essentialist mode of thinking. I would argue that its essential element is the *radicalism* of its attempt to free itself from roots themselves—from the determinations they exert. But I am going to claim that poststructuralism's radicalism is significantly fissured or incomplete. In terms of some of my earlier work, I could say that poststructuralism strives to *escape* the status of the counter-discursive.[1] That is, it seeks to evade any determination that would ventriloquize or pre-script its expression, its "phrasing." It seeks even to avoid the relationship of *negation* of other, constituted discourses. It projects not binding but freeing. But my claim will be that poststructuralism's project has been something like a neurotic or overdetermined reaction to a previously constituted discourse. Or to frame my urging along the lines of an earlier and celebrated call to revolutionary liberation, that this brilliant and salutary latter-day example of the liberatory impulse—I mean poststructuralism—has still to make one more effort to be free. (For this earlier adjuration, see D. A. F. Sade, *La Philosophie dans le boudoir*, 5th dialogue.)

Some people denounce poststructuralism because they claim it is idealist. They argue that poststructuralist thinking resists cognizing, resists responding to developments in what they term the "material" world. By "material world" they seem to mean a world somehow distant from the conceptual, and one that, whatever we think about it, retains some independence from what we think. They would agree that our concepts construct the world for us—of course—but they would resist the notion that such construction is completely free, arbitrary, or under our own control. Poststructuralism they see as too hermetic, too absorbed in its own paradigms, allowing too little of the outside to infiltrate and disturb or drive their development. In effect they condemn poststructuralism for epistemological endogamy, for empirical underdevelopment, for conceptual overdetermination.

The objection I have just formulated against poststructuralism is too simple. I am sure that everyone at this colloquium could neatly deconstruct the opposition between the ideal and the material realms upon which it rests. Yet *something* is being argued in this criticism concerning the thinking of some of our principal interlocutors at this conference. To reframe the denunciation I have put in the mouths of these anti-poststructuralist critics, we might say that poststructuralism has some very definite and very restrictive notions about what forms of relation are acceptable in conceptual discourse—and, more to the point here, about what forms of relation are illegitimate.

Let me begin to test this perception and this critique by turning to the issue that frames our discussion at this colloquium. Today it would seem that the problem of community has a clearly determined conjunctural pertinence—namely, the disappearance of our sense of the collective. Social solidarity seems an idealization from some prelapsarian world, a world we distinctly appear to have lost. So the emergence of our question about community quietly supposes a paradigm of what we used to call *history*.

Critics of poststructuralism would likely argue that, as it has predominantly been framed in some of the work upon which this conference is based, the problem of community is largely an *intralinguistic effect*, that it is the predictable product of certain doctrines operating within the conceptual field of poststructuralism itself. Rather than responding to changes in sociopolitical experience, or in the status or possibility of collective experience, they would claim that the crisis of community as poststructuralists view it is nothing more mysterious than the predictable result of the deep mistrust, within this mode of thinking, concerning *any* category of totality. So, again invoking a pairing whose stability poststructuralists would question, the claim would be that the crisis of community is a deducible effect of certain poststructuralist conceptual proclivities, and has no necessary empirical or sociohistorical basis at all.

On this view, the notion that poststructuralists were responding to developments (as we might say) "in society" would represent a fundamental metalepsis.

We need to ask what would happen if it turned out that our uneasiness about community really represents an adjustment to the suspicion concerning principles of relation that is one of the most characteristic elements in the poststructuralist complex. Would this mean that "historical conjuncture" had nothing to do with it?

In any case, it is clear that our disquiet about community strikingly intertwines with contemporary suspicions concerning *history*. In effect, Jean-Luc Nancy acknowledges and foregrounds this point in the opening paragraph of *La Communauté désoeuvrée*. There we are told that history hardly exists any more. Nancy confidently evokes its exhaustion (11). What is at stake in such a pronouncement?

If we consider the several logics of the differend, of hegemony, even of transgression or of ecstasy, which our principal interlocutors at this conference have offered to help us theorize what they claim is our withered experience of community, they have a common trait: they refuse to countenance the sort of metanarrative or metadiscourse that, as we once naively said, could "bring people together" or "make sense" of history. To our interlocutors here, such explanatory, framing paradigms, and the relations they insist upon, are unacceptable. Thus, in a notion like Jean-François Lyotard's "link"—enchaînement— elements of discourse are conceived as cohering only in terms of the most attenuated form of connection, a kind of zero-degree logic of succession. *Post hoc*, but *never propter hoc*. In this reading, to an extent that may be unprecedented since the High Middle Ages, history is transformed into a narrative of radical parataxis. In poststructuralist diegesis we unexpectedly find ourselves reliving the logic of the *Song of Roland*.

Well, not exactly. For the eleventh century and the *Roland*, meaning was guaranteed by a cultural assumption of the doctrine of the Logos, according to which signs pointed unerringly and unproblematically to their divine referents. So no force of causality or of teleology had to be or really *could* be represented within narrative; all determination flowed from the ineffable world beyond the text, and unceasingly referred it back to such transcendence. This was a world of *parole pleine* to which we can claim no access today. Quoting Thales, Jean-Luc Nancy speaks of a similarly enlarged semiosis in Greek society: *panta plere theon*, "all things full of the gods." And maybe even with a trace of nostalgia Nancy identifies this "uninterrupted world of presences" as responsible for what he terms the greatness (*grandeur*) of the Greeks (124).

In our period, on the other hand, it has come to seem that signs point to nothing at all, or at most only to themselves. Yet unexpectedly the effect is parallel: in the medieval case meaning referred unambiguously to an inaccessible realm by virtue of its absolute transcendence; in the contemporary case there is no longer a division, bridgeable or not, between sign and significance, since— absent the metadiscourse and the extrasemiotic realm—there is no stable significance to begin with. In terms of our old ambitions about history, meaning has become irrelevant, and we are left not with history but with chronicle — with the Lyotardian "link."

In a poignant reappropriation of Bataille, Jean-Luc Nancy evokes this paradigm of an unending, untotalizable succession. In response to our uncertainty concerning community, with Bataille Jean-Luc Nancy tells us that "nous ne pouvons qu'aller plus loin" (68, 102). "We can only go further." This rather Beckettian apothegm we must take as the contemporary version of an answer to Lenin's "What is to be done?" Just go on. But what makes this sentence poignant is Jean-Luc Nancy's *repetition* of it at the conclusion — indeed his repetition of it *is* the conclusion — of *La Communauté désoeuvrée*. What does this iteration do?

Such repetition, such return of the same, effectively subverts any dynamic of temporal flow, of political project, of conceptual *process*, which we might have felt at work in the text. We can only go further. But by literally *repeating* the very sentence that makes the claim, the text subverts it. It seems unable to follow its own injunction. The hortatory tone ("We can only . . .") would appear to project us, but toward what project are we urged? Bataille's project? Nancy's project? Some immanent project joining the two of them and us in some ineffable community? In other words, further than *what*? Essentially this reappropriative, citational move tends to transform the time-sensitive dialectic of social activity — and remember, it is *community* we are worrying about here — into a logic, into tautology. We go on, but our *going* does not *go*. So appropriating the Bataille quotation about going to conclude the text is really a way of enacting stasis. It bleaches out *time*.

Such elision of the diachronic, of the productive character of temporality, is consonant with poststructuralism's claim that the contemporary period has evacuated the discourse of history. Why have we given up history?

History is a *constraint*. Any metadiscourse speaks us, and in a world characterized by increasing programmation and penetration of discourses, we experience any prior scripting, any form of transcendent control, as what Bourdieu would call "symbolic violence" (*Outline of a Theory of Practice*, 191), as an insult, as what I will call a "servitude."

The middle-class ideal of liberty that has animated much of the social project in the period since the French Revolution is thus still very much alive in contemporary theory. As the eighteenth-century revolutionaries sought to be free from feudal exactions, we would like to be free of metadiscourses. But it would be important to ask whether today the project of purging the conceptual realm of its epistemological and ontological servitudes is not a defense, a screen, the cultural or conceptual equivalent of a neurotic substitution, for more intractable social complications. There may be other, less cerebral servitudes, other forms of exaction, that cramp us—though admittedly contesting *them* would involve less cerebral modes of action.

Why do I refuse positivity to the discourses of our prestigious interlocutors at this colloquium, to poststructuralism generally? Why my insistence on considering poststructuralism in its various strains as a rather closely determined counterdiscourse to the concerted historicizing, intensely metadiscursive pretensions of nineteenth-century dialectics? The answer is that I read counterdiscursivity, reactivity, in the very matter of poststructuralism's concepts, and at the very heart of its practices. They are driven by negativity; they define themselves *against*, though they are not always overt in doing so.

Of course the poststructuralists' consciousness of the links between their own protocols and the period of transformation in which we are living, their self-representation, their own metadiscourse if you will, is theoretically no more authoritative than any other. They would argue the point as part of a principled resistance to any constituted authority. Earlier conceptual paradigms, however, would have deprivileged their self-conception for more conjunctural reasons. There is a nice text of Marx's from the preface to *A Contribution to the Critique of Political Economy* that puts this deprivileging strikingly: "Just as one does not judge an individual by what he thinks of himself, so one cannot judge a period of transformation by its consciousness, but, on the contrary, this consciousness must be explained" (21).

So I am tentatively declining the anti-historicist or anti-historical dynamics within poststructuralism. I want to transcode the discourses that assert or practice them in the light of such a refusal. To be sure, such transcoding is not in itself a scandal. On the contrary, the mobility, the *différance* of signs ceaselessly asserts nothing else. But with a flat-footedness for which I apologize, my transcoding reintroduces the kind of metaconsciousness that underlies an assertion of *meaning*. I want to privilege certain forms of relation in a way that violates the practices characteristic of poststructuralism.

The discourse of fundamental forms of relation we could call "logic." The poststructuralist logics that are of concern to us have in common a will to question the forms of relation that can be posited in or about social existence. In such an atmosphere, a regularity emerges clearly. The logic suspicious of community and the logic doubtful of history both call into question fundamental notions or forms of relation. In the case of history, such relations are, broadly speaking, diachronic and deterministic. In the case of community they are, broadly speaking, synchronic and deterministic. The poststructuralist logics before us here wish to deny the pertinence or the validity of forms of relation traditionally posited in the discourses of history and of community. Their object, and their strategy, is to evacuate the category of determination. Under this treatment and *because of it*, important conceptual entities become disabled or *désoeuvrées*: communities collapse and history falls apart.

Some poststructuralists would claim that these effects are *not* simply generated out of the logic that their conceptual practices prescribe. Rather, they would see them as symptomatic of the same developments that led to the generation of such a logic to begin with. In effect, in this view poststructuralism is cast as the consciousness appropriate to our postmodern world. But if we say that, then we are building back into the circuit of admissible relations something like the nineteenth-century explanatory dialectic that on another level poststructuralists refuse. We would be speaking the language of determinism and metadiscourses again.

Perhaps, under poststructuralist assumptions, it makes no sense to ask whether the material world is independent of the conceptual. But the enterprise of philosophy—which we could hardly imagine to be coterminous with the entire conceptual world—is a more local, a more circumscribed phenomenon. We might then ask whether and how philosophy affects or influences social existence and collective experience. Or whether and how it submits to effects from them. If these questions have any sense at all, some further thinking about the kinds of relations that will be admissible in a poststructuralist logic would seem important.

In any case, the questions that brought us together at this colloquium involve an exquisite sensitivity to the phenomenon of relation, and particularly to the arduousness of positing its propriety. This is nowhere more evident than in the intricate rhetorics by which our principal interlocutors here have striven to define or to describe their *own* relation to the historical and conceptual inheritance of the period since the twin revolutions of the nineteenth-century—particularly to Hegel and to Marx.

These adumbrations of linkage with the philosophical and political past are emblematized in what appears as the familiar paradox of a theory—poststructuralism—that writes its relation to its inheritance in terms of a temporalizing prefix ("*post-*"). But the pertinence of this prefix to the relationship described, and the significance of the succession it denotes, are then immediately subverted in the denial that the paradigms of history can any longer produce admissible discourse.

Consider in this light the intricate self-representation by which in their introduction to *Hegemony and Socialist Strategy*, Ernesto Laclau and Chantal Mouffe take the uninflected phrase "post-Marxist" and successively emphasize first one, then the other of its elements (4). The emphasis upon the first of these elements ("*post*-Marxist") in a sense completely undercuts its own assertion, because it supposes meaningful historical succession. It thereby reinscribes the paradigm of determinate supersession that Marxism itself has done the most to articulate. So, saying we are *beyond* Marxism simultaneously but more covertly says we are still deeply *within* Marxism. This seems to me to be why Laclau and Mouffe then immediately go on to reinflect the phrase "post-Marxist." In this second moment they move the emphasis from "post-" to "Marxist." The effect is an attempt to recapture and recontain the paradigmatic and temporal paradox that has been put into play.

In the light of this prickly — I would say counter-discursive — relation to Marxism, to history, and to the dialectic, I think we can say to what experiential and conceptual basis the uneasiness about community corresponds. As I suggested, to postmodern sensibility any form of relation seems to incur the danger of enforcing constraint. Any social relation, once formulated and contracted, takes on a kind of authority or weight that seems to set itself over against the freedom of those who entered into it. Power arises out of relationships and inheres in them.

In this sense, relationships seem *constitutively* and irreducibly historical. If you want to refuse history, refuse relationships. For once they have been posited, agreed to, articulated, mysteriously they seem to enter a world governed by the inexorable unidirectionality of time. In such a world, servitudes analogous to those of the Second Law of Thermodynamics come into play. Everything happens as if entropy determined the social construction and experience of relation. Relations seem to *exceed* logic and *require* history. We see this when we realize that undoing a relation is considerably more problematic than its seemingly free and untrammeled positing would have led one to think. Or, to put it differently, once power is constituted, it is hard to unmake it. Something like minimalist history is implicit in that discovery.

The poststructuralist response is clear. It is to grant every discourse, every moment, every subjectivity the potential of an irreducible singularity, to hold out the privilege of absolute disconnection. No *relationship*, hence no *determination*. On the conceptual level, this move quite neatly reinstitutes freedom. But there are costs. For example, on such a view, how could community *not* be a problem? The object of the move to deny or disable relation is plain, and unquestionably praiseworthy: it is to preserve the rights and the sociopolitical force of alterity, to prevent domination by constituted power or by what some term "legitimate" authority. Against forms of domination, the stakes in such liberatory initiatives are evident. They appear clearly in this passage from Jean-François Lyotard's *Postmodern Condition*:

> The nineteenth and twentieth centuries have given us as much terror as we can take. We have paid a high enough price for the nostalgia of the whole and the one. . . . We can hear the mutterings of the desire for a return to terror, for the realization of the fantasy to seize reality. The answer is: Let us wage war on totality. (81–82)

I would agree that to the extent they carry determinative force, relations always have something like totality as their horizon. This is why, as I have suggested, any relation entails a constraint, a servitude. Yet it is not clear that the duress they imply can be avoided by placing the category of relation itself on some Index of

Prohibited Notions. There may well be an irreducible idealism in attempting to evade determination by seeking to empty out its concept.

It has been argued that the history of Stalinism and the specter of the Gulag are the real determinants of these poststructuralist positions. The quotation from Jean-François Lyotard that I have just cited suggests just this point in a barely coded way. Yet if this is so, it is less clear how appropriate such an intensely counterdiscursive perception of the contemporary political danger may really be. Nonetheless its pervasive and somewhat uncanny force can be sensed in a curious slippage at the beginning of *La Communauté désoeuvrée*. In the opening paragraph of that book, Jean-Luc Nancy strikingly misremembers Sartre's remark concerning the unsurpassable horizon of philosophy in the modern period. In *Questions de méthode* Sartre had referred to Marxism as this horizon. But via a *lapsus* Jean-Luc Nancy replaces "Marxism" with "communism" (11). In a philosopher so exquisitely sensitive to the privileges of difference as Jean-Luc Nancy, it is striking to see precisely *that* difference simply liquidated. The sorry history of the Leninist parties in Western Europe (and in France particularly) cannot give much comfort to the dwindling partisans of what now no doubt appears to us as the Very Old Left. All the less reason to concede to the Comintern the power to decide the course of contemporary Western philosophy.

But the question of community—if not of "communism"—is still before us. I would like to address it briefly. Let me begin by resurrecting the fundamental question Georg Simmel asked in 1908: "How Is Society Possible?" Simmel tried to answer it. Following Vico's distinction between the making of nature and the making of the social world, Simmel observed that, as Kant had asserted, the unity of nature emerges in the observing subject exclusively. But perception of society requires no similar outside, independent observer. Rather, the elements of society, people—who are conscious, synthesizing units—directly realize this unity. And they do so in both senses of "realize": they perceive it, and they create it (7).

You will see that via Simmel and his attribution of a synthesizing capacity to individual perception of the social world, I have smuggled in a metadiscourse, a version of "relation" that I argued earlier many poststructuralists would tend to suspect or to refuse. Perhaps one could put the issue this way: If we strive to preserve the privileges of difference, does this entail abandoning the very possibility of synthesis, of unification—in other words, of community? Here, Ernesto Laclau and Chantal Mouffe implicitly come to my aid in allowing for at least provisional, nonessential, contingent production of such centripetal social and conceptual formations. That is what they call hegemony.

But how can the experience of such hegemony, of such unification, arise? Simmel makes a crucial point. He observes that no one could deny that individuals, the units of such unification, are *organized* by the larger processes of the whole. In my terms here, they are the victims of its servitudes. But Simmel goes on to say that this "causal nexus" that operates upon them is "transformed into a teleological nexus as soon as it is considered from the perspective of . . . individuals" themselves (22). Nor is this assumption by individuals of a program that is determined partly beyond them purely a mystification. Rather, this perspectival transformation is a function of individual consciousness as much as it is a servitude imposed upon it. As Simmel puts it, the process is what "transforms [individual consciousness] into a social element." Community is something I could choose.

Let me conclude by offering a rather unexpected parallel with a different description of the process of individual consciousness. I quote a striking passage on memory from Baudelaire's "Paradis artificiels":

> Entre le palimpseste qui porte, superposées l'une sur l'autre, une
> tragédie grecque, une légende monacale et une histoire de chevalerie, et
> le palimpseste divin créé par Dieu, qui est notre incommensurable
> mémoire, se présente cette différence, que dans le premier il y a comme
> un chaos fantastique, grotesque, une collision entre des éléments
> hétérogènes; tandis que dans le second [la mémoire] la fatalité du
> tempérament met forcément une harmonie entre les éléments les plus
> disparates. Quelque incohérente que soit une existence, l'unité humaine
> n'en est pas troublée. Tous les échos de la mémoire, si on pouvait les
> réveiller simultanément, formeraient un concert, agréable ou
> douloureux, mais logique et sans dissonances. (451)
> [An important difference exists between the palimpsest manuscript
> that superposes, one upon the other, a Greek tragedy, a monastic legend,
> and a chivalric tale, and the divine palimpsest created by God, which
> is our incommensurable memory: in the first there is something like a
> fantastic, grotesque randomness, a collision between heterogeneous
> elements; whereas in the second (memory) the inevitability of
> temperament necessarily establishes a harmony among the most
> disparate elements. However incoherent a given existence may be, its
> human unity is not upset. All the echoes of memory, if one could
> awaken them simultaneously, would form a concert—pleasant or
> painful, but logical and without dissonance (my translation).]

It is evident that this reflection on memory really represents an incipient but quite powerful theory of representation. For memory, as I have argued elsewhere, is the model for any representation, for textuality itself. From the point of view of our discourse at this colloquium and of the problem that frames it, what challenges in this striking quotation is the degree to which Baudelaire in his theory of representation explicitly clotures the free play of codes,[2] and limits the privilege of difference—which, as I have suggested, at least some would claim is responsible for our conceptual difficulties about community to begin with.

What fascinates me in Baudelaire's notion of memory is the progress he makes in adumbrating a *material* basis for a theory of textuality that would also be a theory of consciousness. His notion of consciousness as writing is explicit in the metaphor of the palimpsest. But from his image Baudelaire does not draw the postmodernist conclusion of textual liberation. Rather, he demonstrates the degree to which the stopping of the play of codes and of difference is an *inevitable*, *determined* consequence of the technologies and discourses of consciousness itself.

Texts are theoretically free, of course: anything *might* be written at any time. But in conjuncture, in context, texts are produced by determinate producers and by determinate practices. The crucial point is that whereas textuality has been taken by a number of poststructuralists as the model and the ideal of the unconstrained circulation of codes and signifiers, for Baudelaire textuality is constituted by, governed by a metadiscourse, a metadiscourse of unification—what Simmel called "synthesizing." Baudelaire's perception would suggest that the effort to eradicate such metadiscourses in order to preserve the privileges of untrammelled textuality may be contradictory or even positively delusive.

Baudelaire's assertion about the formation of sense foregrounds the degree to which, *pace* poststructuralism, the establishment of *relation* is essential to language's and to consciousness's process. Unity, community, however problematical, may be more thinkable than we thought.

Notes

1. See my *Discourse/Counter-Discourse: The Theory and Practice of Symbolic Resistance in Nineteenth-Century France* (Ithaca: Cornell University Press, 1985).

2. On the free play of codes, see Roland Barthes, *S/Z*, trans. R. Miller (New York: Hill & Wang, 1974), 140.

Recalling a Community
at Loose Ends

Linda Singer

The writing of community, especially when mobilized by a strategy of critical revision, is a task of retrieving and unraveling loose ends, one's own as well as the multiple and often contradictory significations conjoined or recollected by this collective signifier. It is a task that although it lacks any definitive authorizing foundation, is always already situated, paradigmatically, politically, libidinally, and institutionally. The condition of being situated in the contemporary world order, marked as a "global village" linked by technologies of transport, communication, and information systems that reconfigure spatiotemporal distances and limits, is a complex affair of overdeterminations and polymorphous affiliations. The writing of community under such circumstances both calls and recalls the paradoxical places from which it emerges and toward which it moves.

When I reflect on the situation of this particular writing, I find myself moved to represent it through the feminist and postmodern discursive figures of the fractured subject whose discourse emerges through a play of semiotically coded positions. Whoever or whatever speaks in this text has emerged as a consequence of the variety of positions — geographical, temporal, affective, among others — that I have had occasion to occupy since some of my colleagues at Miami University began to organize the two-year series of events that became known as "Community at Loose Ends." One phase of that process is represented by the essays in this volume, all of which were presented, in some version, at our institution in Oxford, Ohio, during the fall of 1988.

Many of those voices likely "belong" to some of my colleagues at Miami who have been working together for over two years on the dimensions of the "community at loose ends" that cannot be adequately represented or simulated by this volume. What situates this writing but cannot exactly be written is the effect of this proleptic endeavor of trying "to be a community" at the same time that one is also reading and thinking, and writing and talking about it. In practice, this meant that "the Miami chapter" of the community at loose ends, only some of whose contributions are directly represented in this volume, sustained itself as an elective commitment to the pursuit of the question of how to exist as a community devoted to the pursuit of community. Much of what emerged from this process is inscribed in a situationally specific register that does not lend itself to description or prediction, and that cannot be represented on a blueprint or measured for a prescription. Its exchange value may be limited by the fact that it existed in local script, which is never completely transferable. And because, at least in my case, the value of that experience is also registered in a currency of pleasures and resistances that are inseparable from the specificities of their occasion.

Part of what was especially valuable, that is, pleasurable, and at times infuriating about this process for the Miami contingent was that this community at loose ends was one that entailed a commitment of time, energy, and mental space to do work that was not, in any of the ordinary institutional senses, "one's own." This was a community that was, therefore, enabling but also demanding. Its structures both facilitated and expected a commitment both to the solitary discipline of reading and thinking, and to the discipline entailed in getting together periodically to talk and think collectively about what we had read in common. This process, to be sure, was not without its frustrations and struggles. This was after all a group that although from a certain demographic height appeared relatively homogeneous—i.e., mostly white, middle-class intellectuals (students and faculty) from humanities departments—was also defined by and heavily invested in the differences in its members' expertise, institutional positions, ideological affiliations, and political agendas. These differences became objects of deadlock and resentment almost as often as they enabled a provocative semiotic play of positions. As a community in resistance—to hegemonic forms of authority, knowledge, and institutional and discursive practices—it was also a community that produced its own forms of resistance, to which I will return in the concluding statements of this essay.

But at the outset, and with a certain nostalgia, as I reflect on the effect of the community on my thinking about community, I must confess that the dominant register is that of pleasure in the form of a *jouissance* that is specific both to being a community and to being this particular community. Not surprisingly perhaps, this effect became most pronounced for me during the semester when I began writing this piece, which was also a semester in which I was away from the community that I was, at least in some sense, writing for and about. Faced with my own separation from the activities of the group, I became more acutely aware of their significance. The occasion to read in common and speak with each other about what we had read was a significant part of the enterprise of rethinking community, especially in light of the institutional logic of the academy, where one's professional position is justified largely by the fact that there is no one else there reading and studying what you do. Against this background, reading in common with those with whom one also shares an institutional space is powerful and in this case was also provocative. Part of what the activities of this group provoked, beyond some intensive arguments and debates, was a collective sense that the sign of community in this case was not just a discursive object, but also a way of being and doing things collectively in which those party to the discussion and the project in which we were engaging together were also implicated, emotionally and psychically as well as intellectually.

It is this affective sense of a connection that is singular and yet not solitary that I am both recollecting and drawing upon with pleasure as I write this. The specificity and nonrepeatability of this part of the community at loose ends will, I suspect, continue to connect those who were a part of it in ways that will never be fully articulate to any of us, but will nonetheless continue to haunt and appeal to us. It is also that which this text hopes somehow to commemorate, as a gesture of gratitude for a gift that cannot be repaid in kind, both to our guests and to those with whom I continue to work. Their voices can also be heard in this essay, and in the others in this volume.

Although our discussions were marked by a certain local specificity, they might also be situated within the more general paradigmatic frameworks marked by another contemporary collective signifier, that of "postmodernism." Although that signifier suffers from a certain vagueness, and is often used to abridge important differences between the viewpoints collected under it, the form our discussions took, the questions we asked and the issues that emerged as sites of contest, bore the influence of theory and aesthetics in which any gestures of preemptive totalization and condensation are already problematized, and in which much of the traditional rhetoric associated with discussions of community has already been placed under erasure.

This discussion is also informed by a critical sensibility in which the discursive and political potency, legitimacy, and utility of the language of community is not and cannot be taken for granted because so many of the other signs and concepts that have historically been appropriated as part of its articulatory apparatus have also been put in question. Since deconstructive readings have problematized the mechanisms of closure that have traditionally produced unified, coherent, rational subjects and societies, dissolving them into semiotically localized plays of differences, the strategic and conceptual function played by the notion of community must also, as a consequence, be recast. In a postmodern context, the problematic of community is no longer that of articulating the possible conditions for the formation of a collective will or state of being capable of superseding or supplementing a situation in which individuated subjects are already particularized through placement in a grid of oppositional distinctions. Nor can community be figured as a mark of a state of grace already given to those with being in common as consequences of a common origin or nature. Absent the foundational terms that have traditionally functioned as its markers, community in the postmodern world is a far more complex and ambivalent signifier, linked not only with need and desire, but also with the forces of resistance and denial.

In the discourse of Western metaphysics, concepts of community emerge within a logic of bipolarity in which the language of collectivity is paired as the opposing or supplemental term with respect to individuals or particulars. Within such a dualistic framework, the function of community has largely been that of managing, consolidating, or overriding the dissembling effects of a *non*regulated interplay of differences. The maintenance of order through appeal to the collective is as vital to Plato's republic as it is to Kant's kingdom of ends. Within the oppositional logic of individuals and universals, the problem of community is cast largely as a problem of genesis, which seeks the modes of affiliation, copresence, and identification that could emerge, or that already serve to bind this collection of already autonomous and atomistically related particulars.

This way of posing the problem of community initiates a particular agenda with respect to the representation and positioning of differences. Differences are what this concept of community is intended to overcome. As two hegemonic formations constitutive of our contemporary conception of community, Christianity and liberalism represent historical efforts to initiate visions of a social order founded on a model of community in which differences are harmoniously sutured or drastically diminished in their effect and significance. Whether through appeal to a myth of common origins in God or to the natural order, to preestablished harmonies, human nature, or social contracts—to name but a few of the apparati nominated for this function—the effect of these hegemonic formations of community has been to solidify a logic of sameness with respect to that which it also collects, while concealing or mystifying the mechanisms by which this effect is produced.

For both Christianity and liberalism, the economy proposed for the elimination of difference is the economy of presence. But as with all such recuperative gestures, they also work to reactivate that which they exile or repress. Hence the logic of difference reasserts itself within the logic of community, not as a representation of presence, but as a supplemental difference that emerges from its circulation, its exchange, its writing. As a result of its circulatory recurrence in a range of sociometaphysical paradigms, the sign of community is infected with a certain elasticity that resubjects community to a range of projects and strategies. The term circulates promiscuously through a variety of discourses—often with the effect of muddying the ideological waters. One may find appeals to community as an authorizing force of exclusion, when the U.S. Supreme Court uses the language of ''community standards'' as the basis on which particular cultural artifacts may be removed from circulation. One may hear in the totalizing discourses associated with hegemonic forms of authority the appropriation of community as a way of marginalizing the effects of structuring difference, like race, gender, and class, precisely in order to pacify those disadvantageously positioned by those differences. Both presidential candidates in the recent election were careful to remind Americans that "we are all one" — even as government statistics demonstrated the widening economic gaps among us. Similar rhetoric is often associated with advocacy groups like the Chamber of Commerce.

But ironically, the term that is supposed to supersede the disruptive effects of difference can also be appropriated for discourses of differentiation. When gays, blacks, and feminists, for example, appeal to the notion of community as part of a movement rhetoric or on their own behalf, that appeal takes the form of a demand, a demand for the recognition of differences and the systematic asymmetries they produce. For a member of a marginalized group, the invocation of community marks an existentially and politically vital site of affiliation, and a refusal of false inclusion or erasure.

Community can be offered as an object of appeasement or incitement, aspiration or accomplishment, because it is also an object of appeal, not called in its presence but rather addressed proleptically in its absence. The elasticity of community is its appeal, an appeal that operates not as presence but as discourse, exchange, and difference. The elasticity of community as an overdetermined cultural sign allows for its circulation as a common element of the Western social imaginary, independent of any consensus about its signification. That is because community is not a referential sign but a call or appeal. What is called for is not some objective reference. The call of community aims at response, a calling back. The call of community initiates a conversation, prompts exchanges in writing, disseminates, desires the proliferation of discourse.

When one reads the appeal to community in this way, as the call of something other than presence, the problematic posed by the prospect of community shifts to the economy of discourse and articulation. Within the framework of this dispersive episteme, the question of community is less a matter of organizational logistics or normative consolidations, and more a problematic framed within the strategic dynamics of writing. As a result, the thinker is confronted with somewhat different questions. How, and for whom, does one write of community? From where, or on what basis, does one write? How can one represent the possibility of sociocorporeal totalities in an era of antitotalization? How can community be represented without occluding the very economy of differences upon which writing and articulatory exchange depend?

The variety of idiolects and conceptual strategies taken by the essays that form this community at loose ends indicates that there is much more at stake than a choice between rhetorics and voices and fetishized differences. When community is considered as an intertextual construct with a contradictory and ambiguous history, the questions of how and for what purpose one now chooses to write of it, and what form such writing should assume, confront the writer with a complex nexus of positional choices. In attempting to write community, should one be operating within the genre of myth, producing a discourse of desire that proceeds on the basis of the lack or absence of that which is called for by the writing? Or is one producing a retrospective commemorative narrative, a writing after the fact? Is the sign of community to be deployed as a descriptive concept, marking something factical, given not as a matter of choice or effort but rather as a dynamic that is situationally conditional? Or is the sign of community to be used as a marker along a normative continuum, and therefore represented in the language of what ought or ought not be? Is community to be figured as that which can be celebrated or strived for as an antidote to alienation and subjugation? Or ought it be challenged for its politics of false inclusion, its denial of difference, and its utility as an apparatus of hegemony? Should the writing of community work to facilitate or obstruct the formation of community in thought and practice?

The essays collected in this volume have reached no consensus, nor did they aim at producing some discursive resolution. But the points of contention between them indicate that resituating the problem of community within a discursive economy does not displace political questions, but reposes them in other registers, among them the registers of intertextual histories of authority and the legitimation of power through knowledge. The epistemic problematic of community emerges as a problem of legitimacy and entitlements. From where arises the authority to constitute the ''we'' of community, and what position is assumed by the agent or apparatus of this constitution? Is the discourse that writes community a performative in which the forms of collective affiliation connoted by community are produced in the very gesture of naming? Within the framework of an epistemics of difference, on what grounds is one entitled to evoke the sign of that which supersedes difference? What is the relation between power and knowledge assumed by such writing, and how ought its consequences be gauged?

Because community can function as an authorizing signifier, a circulator of authority, and is also that in terms of which demands can be made and claims to entitlement staked or avoided, it has assumed a certain importance for critical discourses, like Marxism, which seek to intervene in the hegemonic construction of authority. The signifier ''communism'' functions in Marxist discourse as a critical disruption of the dominant myths of community that legitimate the maintenance of an oppressive system of differences. Communism is represented as the alternative to the kind of community that works as a form of mystification and hence as an impediment to the recognition of class struggle. Marxism provides an account of the origins of the myth of community in the needs created by a system in which labor is alienated and human relationships are governed by laws of competitive individualism, possession, and exploitation. Because individuation is produced as a consequence of social relationships of domination, individuation emerges as a form of suffering from which one seeks relief, salvation. It is the persistence of the conditions that produce this need that helps account for the perpetuation of visions of community that are clearly counterfactual, but continue to speak to the proleptic logic of desire. Marxism offers the myth of "communism" as alternative and antidote, as a way of organizing human needs for affinity under the sign of a liberatory revolution, and as a visionary position from which to engage in a systematic critique of existing social relationships.

For some time, especially in a European context, Marxism has been the dominant discourse for circulating community as a critical, revolutionary signifier. It is precisely the hegemony of this idiolect and its specific articulatory apparatus that may have prompted several of the contributors to position their discourses as "post-Marxist." Such a designation asserts an unwillingness to be bound by Marxism's particular mythology, metaphysics, and rhetoric, as well as casting a critical regard on the social movements that have been carried out under the banner of communism. But I think it is a misreading to assume that such a designation marks a site of refusal, an unwillingness to engage the political consequences of the effort to revise a sign as central to our social imaginary as is the sign of community, despite Lyotard's ironic cast on political enthusiasms. The appropriation of Marxism as that which is to be superseded already situates many of these essays within a politically marked space in which Marxism is but one form of articulating revisionist impulses.

If decentering Marxism as the privileged progressive narrative is a crime, then that crime committed by postmodernism cannot be read as one of betrayal, especially since much of the postmodern reading of Marxism as a mythology appropriates and recuperates many of the strategies used by Marxists in their ironic readings of bourgeois social narratives. The refusal to grant regulatory status to Marxist rhetoric ought not be read as tantamount to a refusal of politics as such, as if such a thing were even possible. This refusal is better read as a political strategy, which has, as one of its effects, the reopening of the political as a site of discursive contestation. Because such contestation does not depend on privileged access to some form of knowledge, presence, or consciousness, its epistemic economy moves in the direction of disseminating sites of intervention, and hence decentralizing authority. The strategic effect of politicizing discourse is not to truncate the political but rather to force attention to the political mechanisms by which the political is historically produced as a socially legitimated discourse.

Part of what is at stake in the postmodernist critique of Marxism's image of community entails a dispute over epistemic politics, specifically the rejection of the notion of privileged positions, consciousness, or states of being, presumed by the Marxist narrative of "revolutionary liberation," as well as by the methodology of dialectical materialism.

Part of what may also motivate opposition to the Marxist conception of community is a desire to differentiate discursive politics from the mythology of the revolutionary vanguard, a position second-generation Marxists like Lenin assigned to writers and theorists. In the classical formulation of second-generation Marxists, the vanguard is the ideological arm of revolutionary struggle charged with the historical mission of generating the signs through which the proletariat's emerging class consciousness can recognize and articulate itself. Part of the vanguard's historical mission is to instigate a counterculture capable of displacing the reified mystifications produced by the ruling class. As the mediator between the historically specific position of the revolutionary class and the liberatory position toward which they are to be moved, the vanguard stands in a relationship of transcendence and relative privilege with respect both to the conditions that motivate their discursive production and to the destinations of that production. The vanguard operates in Marxist theory with the authority ascribed to those who can articulate the mechanisms of false consciousness because they also enjoy the epistemic power of transcendence over them. The vanguard can act as free agents, as historically underdetermined, because they somehow avoid subjugation by that which they disclose and resist.

If this is one of the myths in terms of which a community of critical theorists is formed, it is also one from which many theorists identified with a postmodernist politics of knowledge, as well as with movements on behalf of oppressed or marginalized people, would want to dissociate themselves. As one who is both identified with and has been politically educated by these struggles against domination, I have been moved by the writing emerging from these movements that has pointed to the contradiction between Marxism's liberationist rhetorics and its imaginary of social transformation through mastery, dialectical or otherwise. Anyone who has ever been silenced because he or she is female or gay or black or poor would likely, as I do, want to resist the idea that some speech is intrinsically privileged, epistemically, historically, or otherwise. Anyone who has operated from a position marked as marginal needs, at some level, to resist the reification of historical positioning, and its normalization through the authority of knowledge. If such differences of access to authority exist, and they do, the mythology that elevates these differences to the order of being, to an indication of having been chosen for the grace of privileged access, must be resisted strategically, not as false consciousness, but as bad politics, i.e., politics that recuperates its own mythic resistances and then misrecognizes them as liberatory strategies.

One site of resistance to the politics of mastery has come from the literature of struggle against oppression, which contests the terms in which the boundaries of the political have been hegemonically overdetermined, as well as from the critical interventions of postmodernism into the hegemonic politics of knowledge. When feminists insist the "the personal is political," such discourse works to intervene in the mechanisms that construct the political as a specific apparatus and expertise to which only some, by definition, will ever have access, whether by choice or necessity. The contention that the personal is political politically contests that construction, in part, with a different political imaginary, one in which the political community is not that which is entered electively, hence also that which one can refuse or resist, but a nonnegotiable consequence of our being in relation and in difference.

If the personal is political, so is that which has been generated as its correlate. If the personal is political, so is the call of community. It is not a call that can be refused, in the ordinary sense, but a nonnegotiable consequence of our being together. The political imaginary of community set in motion by this kind of political intervention is not that of another long forced march. Less a politics dependent on the mythology of mass mobilization, the political resistance I am associating with antiauthoritarian struggles like feminism is one dependent on mechanisms of dissemination as well as condensation, inscription as well as conscription. In recasting the political relationship between the personal and that which the personal is designed to resist, a critical intervention is made into the contemporary political economy of knowledge, as well as into the hegemonic social imaginary of those positioned by and invested in it. Addressing intellectuals in a way that already implicates them in a communal context tends to disrupt the hegemonic mythology of a community of thinkers related only as independent dissociated points of view whose value and integrity are defined by the maintenance and fetishizing of differences, particularly those attached to a system of subjects fixed by proper names. This disruption has the effect of occasioning the articulation of a certain form of resistance to the idea of community, a resistance situated in a counterimaginary, that is, a different narrative of what community portends for thinkers.

There is much in the contemporary political economy of knowledge and its system of competitive merit that encourages resistance to the kinds of affiliation suggested by the language of community. In the system of rewards governing contemporary scholarship, value is assessed and privileges distributed according to codes of originality and singularity, that is, by the work's capacity to set itself apart. This political economy is also buttressed by the romantic narrative of the thinker as the one who stands outside the community, as its gadfly, conscience, or prophet. It is a tale as old as Socrates, but one that has been progressively elaborated and reinvented by legendary figures like Nietzsche, Heidegger, and Derrida. It is a story that encourages the thinker to assume a position toward what exists in common that is exclusively alienated, and that addresses it only to destabilize it through critique, disruption, or deconstruction. It is a theme with many variations. One version, initiated by thinkers like Thoreau, Emerson, and Rand, constitutes the sphere of commonality as that which promises false comforts and threatens loss of vision, ingenuity, and power. The heroic thinker is the one who maintains the integrity of his isolation, and whose stature and authority arise from his refusal of association, his willingness to stand alone. This figure sets in motion an imaginary ideal of intellectual independence that is metaphorized solipsistically, and where the common is only that which is to be overcome, or at least resisted.

The writings collected in this volume address this intellectual imaginary in a way that forms a community of resistance with other antiauthoritarian discourses and struggles. The community at loose ends works against this elective refusal of the common by insisting on its differences in ways that disrupt the circuitry by which the call of community is made and heard, especially by those engaged in the production of cultural signs, which is largely as a call for the denial of difference. Rather than a disciplinary call to mass mobilization, the community at loose ends seduces by its looseness, its willingness to exhibit its differences face to face, in public and in print. This insistence on the conspicuous display of differences works to frustrate and resist any political imaginary founded on mastery, any myth of the common as that which solidifies authority. This strategic display of difference is excessive with respect to a hegemonic political economy in which knowledge is linked with the production of social utilities and the consolidation of authority through the reification of signs and the mass mobilizations of populations around them. For some readers, this promiscuous excess may read as a form of decadence incompatible with a political imaginary founded on models of mastery and organizational discipline. They will want to resist the forms of community-in-complicity that they are being called to recognize. They will want to resist the disseminative imaginary of writing that calls in the form of seduction.

Others, like me, will be seduced into complicity with this effort to reinvent some of our social imaginaries, this disseminative invitation in the call-and-response mode. The appeal of the community at loose ends from where I think and write is that in that very thought and writing, I am already also placed in community with that which also calls and responds in this text. This allows me to begin to imagine a way of speaking and writing community that can recognize itself in all those moments in which my being with others, in relation and differences, is what speaks in me, is what allows me to speak of me and the other. I imagine a call of community that appeals across differences along more promiscuous and disseminative circuits than are currently available. I imagine a speaking of community that speaks in the voice of the other, and is better capable of understanding, appreciating, celebrating what that means.

I refuse to live and create from a defensive position. I write to fight.
— Ntozake Shange

Works Cited

Anson, Bert. *The Miami Indians*. Norman: University of Oklahoma Press, 1970.

Arendt, Hannah. "Totalitarian Organization." In *The Origins of Totalitarianism*. Rev. ed. New York: Harcourt, Brace and World, 1966: 364–88.

Barber, Benjamin. *Strong Democracy*. Berkeley: University of California Press, 1984.

Barthes, Roland. *S/Z*. Trans. R. Miller. New York: Hill & Wang, 1974.

Baudelaire, Charles. *Les Paradis artificiels*. In *Oeuvres complètes*. Ed. Y.-G. Le Dantec and Claude Pichois. Paris: Gallimard-Pléiade, 1961.

Berlin, Isaiah. "Two Concepts of Liberty." In *Four Essays on Liberty*. Oxford: Oxford University Press, 1969.

Blanchot, Maurice. "Le Communisme sans héritage." *Revue Comité* 1968. Rpt. in *Gramma* 3/4 (1976): 31–33.

Bobbio, Norberto. *The Future of Democracy*. Trans. R. Griffin. Minneapolis: University of Minnesota Press, 1987.

Boswell, James. *Life of Johnson*. Ed. George Birkbeck Hill and L. F. Powell. 6 vols. Oxford: Clarendon, 1934–50.

Bourdieu, Pierre. *Outline of a Theory of Practice*. Trans. R. Nice. Cambridge, Mass.: Harvard University Press, 1977.

Carter, Harvey Lewis. *The Life and Times of Little Turtle, First Sagamore of the Wabash*. Urbana and Chicago: University of Illinois Press, 1987.

Cixous, Hélène. "La Crise dans la littérature." *Les Lettres françaises* 221 (November 25–30, 1970).

——— . *Manne*. Paris: Des Femmes, 1988.

Deleuze, Gilles, and Félix Guattari. *Mille Plateaux*. Paris: Minuit, 1980.

Derrida, Jacques. "Paul de Man's War." Trans. P. Kamuf. *Critical Inquiry* 14 (1988): 590–652.

——— . "Signature Event Context." In *Limited Inc*. Trans. S. Weber and J. Mehlmann. Evanston: Northwestern University Press, 1988.

Downing, David B. "Deconstruction's Scruples: The Politics of Enlightened Critique." *Diacritics* 17, 3 (Fall 1987): 66–81.

Fraisse, Geneviève. *Muse de la Raison: La démocratie exclusive et la différence des sexes*. Aix-en-Provence: Alinea, 1989.

Frege, Gottlob. "On Sense and Reference." Trans. M. Black. *Translations from the Philosophical Writings*. 2nd ed. Ed. Peter Geach and Max Blacks. Oxford: Basil Blackwell, 1960: 56–78.

Fynsk, Christopher. "Freiheit der Interpretation im liberalen Amerika." Trans. Thomas Kleinbub. *Tumult*. Munich: Klaus Boer, 1987: 125–32.

Geras, Norman. "Post-Marxism?" *New Left Review* 163 (1987): 40–82.

Gramsci, Antonio. *Prison Notebooks*. New York: International Publishers, 1971.

Habermas, Jürgen. *The Philosophical Discourse of Modernity: Twelve Lectures*. Trans. F. G. Lawrence. Cambridge, Mass.: MIT Press, 1987.

Hegel, Georg Wilhelm Friedrich. *Phenomenology of Mind*. Trans J. B. Baillie. New York: Harper & Row, 1967.

Heidegger, Martin. *Being and Time*. Trans. John Macquarrie and Edward Robinson. New York: Harper & Row, 1962.

――――. *Die Selbstbehauptung der deutschen Universität*. Breslau: Korn, 1933.

――――. "What Is Metaphysics?" Trans. David Farrell Krell. *Basic Writings*. New York: Harper & Row, 1977.

Horkheimer, Max, and Theodor Adorno. *Dialectics of Enlightenment*. Trans. J. Cumming. New York: Seabury, 1972.

Husserl, Edmund. *Cartesian Meditations*. Trans. D. Cairns. The Hague: Nijhoff, 1964.

Irigaray, Luce. "Le Sexe linguistique." *Languages* 85, 21 (March 1987).

Jameson, Fredric. "Of Islands and Trenches: Neutralization and the Production of Utopian Discourse." *Diacritics* 7, 2 (1977): 2–21. Rpt. in *The Ideologies of Theory*. 2 vols. Minneapolis: University of Minnesota Press, 1988. II: 75–101.

Kant, Immanuel. "An Old Question Raised Again: Is the Human Race Constantly Progressing?" Part 2 of *The Conflict of the Faculties*. Trans. R. Anchor. *On History*. Ed. Lewis White Beck. Indianapolis: Bobbs-Merrill, 1963: 137–54.

Kripke, Saul. *Naming and Necessity*. Cambridge, Mass.: Harvard University Press, 1972.

Kristeva, Julia. *Au Commencement était l'amour. Psychanalyse et foi*. Paris: Hachette, coll. Textes du XXe siècle, 1985. Translated by Arthur Goldhammer, *In the Beginning Was Love: Psychoanalysis and Faith*. New York: Columbia University Press. 1987.

Laclau, Ernesto. *Politics and Ideology in Marxist Theory*. London: New Left Books, 1977.

――――. "Metaphor and Social Antagonisms." *Marxism and the Interpretation of Culture*. Ed. L. Grossberg and C. Nelson. Urbana: University of Illinois Press, 1988: 249–57.

Laclau, Ernesto, and Chantal Mouffe. *Hegemony and Socialist Strategy: Towards a Radical Democratic Politics*. Trans. W. Moore and P. Cammack. London: Verso, 1985.

――――. "Post-Marxism without Apologies." *New Left Review* 166 (1987): 78–106.

Lacoue-Labarthe, Philippe. Introduction to Walter Benjamin, *Le Concept de critique esthétique dans le romantisme allemand*. Paris: Flammarion, 1986.

Lefort, Claude. *The Political Forms of Modern Society: Bureaucracy, Democracy, Totalitarianism*. Trans. and ed. J. B. Thompson. Oxford: Oxford University Press, 1986.

Leibniz, Gottfried W. "Discourse on Metaphysics." Trans. and ed. Leroy Loemker. *Philosophical Papers and Letters*. 2nd ed. Dordrecht: Reidel, 1969: 303–30.

Loraux, Nicole. "L'Ame de la cité." *L'Ecrit du temps* 14–15 (1987): 35–54.

Lyotard, Jean-François. *The Differend: Phrases in Dispute*. Trans. G. Van Den Abbeele. Minneapolis: University of Minnesota Press, 1988.

――――. *Heidegger and "the jews."* Trans. A. Michel and M. S. Roberts. Minneapolis: University of Minnesota Press.

――――. "Interview." Questions and trans. by G. Van Den Abbeele. *Diacritics* 14, 3 (1984): 16–21.

_____ . "Judiciousness in Dispute, or Kant after Marx." Trans. C. Lindsay. Ed. Murray Krieger. *The Aims of Representation: Subject/Text/History*. New York: Columbia University Press, 1987: 23–67.

_____ . *Peregrinations: Law, Form, Event*. New York: Columbia University Press, 1988.

_____ . *The Postmodern Condition: A Report on Knowledge*. Trans. Geoff Bennington and Brian Massumi. Minneapolis: University of Minnesota Press, 1984.

Lyotard, Jean-François, and Jean-Loup Thébaud. *Just Gaming*. Trans. W. Godzich. Minneapolis: University of Minnesota Press, 1985.

Marin, Louis. *Utopiques: jeux d'espaces*. Paris: Minuit, 1973.

Marshall, T. H. "Citizenship and Social Class." In *Sociology at the Crossroads*. London: Heinemann, 1963.

Marx, Karl. *A Contribution to the Critique of Political Economy*. Trans. S. W. Ryazanskaya. New York: International Publishers, 1970.

Marx, Karl, and Friedrich Engels. *Manifesto of the Communist Party*. In *Basic Writings on Politics and Philosophy*. Ed. Lewis S. Feuer. Garden City, N.Y.: Doubleday, 1959: 1–41.

Mouffe, Chantal. "American Liberalism and Its Critics: Rawls, Taylor, Sandel and Walzer." Trans. W. Falcetano. *Praxis International* 8, 2 (July 1988): 193–206.

_____ . "Hegemony and New Political Subjects: Toward a New Concept of Democracy." In *Marxism and the Interpretation of Culture*. Ed. L. Grossberg and C. Nelson. Urbana: University of Illinois Press, 1988: 89–101.

Naming the Names. Dir. Stuart Burge. With Sylvestra Le Touzel. Film produced for the British Broadcasting Company, 1986. Aired BBC2, February 8, 1987.

Nancy, Jean-Luc. *La Communauté désoeuvrée*. Paris: Christian Bourgois, 1986. English edition, *The Inoperative Community*. Ed. Peter Connor, trans. Peter Connor, Lisa Garbus, Michael Holland, and Simona Sawhney. Minneapolis: University of Minnesota Press, 1991.

Neumann, Franz L. *Behemoth: The Structure and Practice of National Socialism, 1933–1944*. 2nd Ed. New York: Octagon, 1963.

Oakeshott, Michael. *On Human Conduct*. Oxford: Oxford University Press, 1975.

O'Gorman, Edmundo. *The Invention of America: An Inquiry into the Historical Nature of the New World and the Meaning of Its History*. Bloomington: Indiana University Press, 1961.

Pateman, Carole. *The Sexual Contract*. Stanford, Calif.: Stanford University Press, 1988.

Peirce, Charles Sanders. *Elements of Logic. Collected Papers*. 8 vols. Ed. Charles Hartshorne and Paul Weiss. Cambridge, Mass.: Harvard University Press, 1931–60.

Rawls, John. *A Theory of Justice*. Oxford: Oxford University Press, 1971.

_____ . "The Idea of an Overlapping Consensus." *Oxford Journal of Legal Studies* 7, 1 (Spring 1987): 1–25.

Rorty, Richard. *Contingency, Irony, and Solidarity*. Cambridge, Mass.: Harvard University Press, 1989.

_____ . *Philosophy and the Mirror of Nature*. Princeton: Princeton University Press, 1979.

_____ . *Consequences of Pragmatism*. Minneapolis: University of Minnesota Press, 1982.

_____ . "Habermas, Lyotard et la postmodernité." Trans. F. Latraverse. *Critique* 40 (March 1984): 181–97.

_____ . "Le Cosmopolitisme sans émancipation: en reponse à Jean-François Lyotard." Trans. P. Saint-Amand. *Critique* 41 (March 1985): 569–80.

_____ . "Solidarité ou objectivité." Trans. F. Latraverse. *Critique* 39 (December 1983): 923–40.

Sade, D. A. F. *La Philosophie dans le boudoir*. Ed. Y Belaval. Paris: Gallimard, 1976.

Said, Edward. *The World, the Text, and the Critic*. Cambridge, Mass.: Harvard University Press, 1983.

Sandel, Michael. *Liberalism and the Limits of Justice*. Cambridge, Mass.: Harvard University Press, 1982.

Sartre, Jean-Paul. *Critique de la raison dialectique, précédé de Questions de méthode*. Paris: Gallimard, 1960.

Schmitt, Carl. *The Concept of the Political*. Trans. George Schwab. New Brunswick, N.J.: Rutgers University Press, 1976.

Simmel, Georg. "How Is Society Possible?" In *On Individuality and Social Forms*. Ed. Donald Levine. Chicago: University of Chicago Press, 1971.

Skinner, Quentin. "The Idea of Negative Liberty: Philosophical and Historical Perspective." *Philosophy in History*. Ed. R. Rorty, J. B. Schneewind, and Q. Skinner. Cambridge, Mass.: Harvard University Press, 1984.

Smith, Paul. *Discerning the Subject*. Minneapolis: University of Minnesota Press, 1988.

Taylor, Charles. *Philosophy and the Human Sciences. Philosophical Papers* 2. Cambridge, Mass.: Harvard University Press, 1955.

Terdiman, Richard. *Discourse/Counter-Discourse: The Theory and Practice of Symbolic Resistance in Nineteenth-Century France*. Ithaca, N.Y.: Cornell University Press, 1985.

Todorov, Tzvetan. *The Conquest of America: The Question of the Other*. Trans. R. Howard. New York: Harper & Row, 1984.

Touraine, Alain. *Return of the Actor*. Minneapolis: University of Minnesota Press, 1988.

Verrazzanno, Giovanni da. *Relation du voyage de la Dauphine, A François Ier, roi de France* (1524). In *Les Français en Amérique pendant la première moitié du XVIe siècle*. Ed. René Herval and Charles-André Julien. Paris: PUF, 1946: 51–76.

Wiesel, Elie. *Night*. Trans. S. Rodway. New York: Hill & Wang, 1960.

Wittgenstein, Ludwig. "Lecture on Ethics." *Philosophical Review* 74 (1929–30): 3–27.

_____ . "Remarks of December 30, 1929." Transcribed by Friedrich Waismann. In *Heidegger and Modern Philosophy*. Trans. and ed. Michael Murray. New Haven: Yale University Press, 1978.

Wittig, Monique. *Virgile-non*. Paris: Minuit, 1988.

Wood, Ellen Meiksins. *The Retreat from Class*. London: Verso, 1986.

Contributors

The Miami Theory Collective is based in the department of French and Italian at Miami University in Oxford, Ohio, but also includes members from other areas of knowledge. The Collective sponsors sustained and focused dialogue on issues it considers significant to contemporary discourse. For this volume on community the Collective includes James Creech, Mitchell Greenberg, Britton Harwood, Peggy Kamuf, Stephen Nimis, Marie-Claire Vallois, and Georges Van Den Abbeele.

Verena Andermatt Conley is professor of French at Miami University. She is the author of *Hélène Cixous: Writing the Feminine* (1984) and is the editor of Cixous's *Reading with Clarice Lispector* (1990).

Christopher Fynsk is associate professor of comparative literature at SUNY at Binghamton. He is the author of *Heidegger: Thought and Historicity* (1986) and the editor of *Typography: Mimesis, Philosophy, Politics* (1989).

Peggy Kamuf is professor of French at the University of Southern California and is the author of *Fictions of Feminine Desire* (1982) and *Signature Pieces* (1988).

Ernesto Laclau is the director of the graduate program in ideology and discourse analysis at the University of Essex. He is the author of *Politics and Ideology in Marxist Theory* (1977) and *New Reflections on the Revolution of Our Time* (1989), and coauthor, with Chantal Mouffe, of *Hegemony and Socialist Strategy* (1985).

Jean-François Lyotard teaches at the University of Paris (X) and is a visiting professor at the University of California at Irvine. Among his many books are *The Postmodern Condition* (1984), *The Differend* (1988), *Just Gaming* (with Jean-Loup Thébaud), and *Heidegger and "the jews"* (1990).

Chantal Mouffe teaches at the University of London and is the editor of *Gramsci* *and Marxist Theory* and the coauthor, with Ernesto Laclau, of *Hegemony and Socialist Strategy* (1985).

Jean-Luc Nancy teaches at the University of Human Sciences of Strasbourg, France. Among his many books and articles are *L'Expérience de la liberté*, "Sharing Voices" in *Transforming Hermeneutics*, and "Finite History" in *States of Theory* (1989). He is also the coauthor (with Philippe Lacoue-Labarthe) of *The Literary Absolute* (1988).

Linda Singer was associate professor of philosophy at Miami University.

Paul Smith is associate professor in the literary and cultural studies program at Carnegie-Mellon University. He is the author of *Pound Revisited* (1983) and *Discerning the Subject* (1988), and the coeditor, with Alice Jardine, of *Men in Feminism* (1987).

Richard Terdiman teaches French at the University of California at Santa Cruz and is the author of *Discourse/Counter-Discourse* (1985).

Georges Van Den Abbeele is associate professor of French at Miami University. He is the translator of Jean-François Lyotard's *The Differend* (1988), as well as the author of *Travel as Metaphor: From Montaigne to Rousseau* (forthcoming from the University of Minnesota Press).

Index